INSIGHTS AND INSPIRATIONS:
Real-Life Stories From Camp Staff

Michael Jacobus

ISBN: 978-1-60679-377-0
Library of Congress Control Number: 2016962919
Book layout: Cheery Sugabo
Cover design: Cheery Sugabo

Healthy Learning
P.O. Box 1828
Monterey, CA 93942
www.healthylearning.com

We don't do what we do for the income,

We do it for the outcome!

ACKNOWLEDGMENTS

A huge thanks to all these amazing camp professionals who took the time to contribute to this project:

CAMPERS

Cassie Turner

Becky Leary

Kevin J. Costin

Jenny Wilder

Catherine Gorecki

Lisa Merlotti

Fabio Del Carlo

Stuart Jones

James Ferrigan

Lupine Reppert

Danny Sudman

Cheryl Oliveria

Staci Lane

Sergio Medrano

Lani Connolly

STAFF

TJ Roberts

Jamie Yarow

Amanda Zoellner

Ian Moorhouse

Todd Walker

Donna Johns-Thomas

THE BLOGOSPHERE

Sydney Collins

Taylor Zavodnick

Sydney Sutton

Mary Rom

Amanda Bohlmann

Gabi Bon Durant

DIRECTORS

Sarah Resch

Jenny McMillian

Erin Johnson

Sara & Gwynn Powell

Sherri Pacitto

Dale Decker

CAMP SIZANANI

Phil Lilienthal

Kabelo (KayBee)

Malefane

FOREWORD

Camp saves lives.

What a grandiose statement, right? But, if you're not yet convinced … you soon will be. This book details several of the truths of counselors, campers, parents, and the many people who make camp possible. While those truths include memories and emotions, all are marked in some way by a true transformation.

Every camp audience I've ever stood in front of endorses this statement as fact. We all know people—most of us are people—who credit camp with making them the person they are, with giving them the perspective or skills or beliefs that allowed them to thrive. More than that, though, we've all known (and some of us are) people who genuinely would not have made it without camp.

Camp changes every person who attends. As an only child who headed off to overnight camp alone at the age of nine, I learned what it meant to risk. Risk talking to new kids; risk asking questions about traditions that I didn't yet know; risk sharing ideas, space, and fears, and even a cubby.

That first summer was maybe the worst of my life, which is why mom was astounded by my insistence on going back. Nonetheless, back I went that second summer, as well as five more as a camper.

Subsequently, I learned that real change happens when you're responsible for the campers and not just one of them! I've been a camp counselor, unit head, head staff, and camp doctor. In fact, the ultimate proof of my belief in the power of camp … as I write this book, is the fact that all four of my own kids are at their overnight camp, about to head home after three weeks.

So why this book?

In it, you will find your own stories … of talking to a parent about a camper who made your day, only to realize afterward that it was their kid you were talking about. The camper who is, at first, kept awake by the quiet. The 13-year-old boys who impress all the adults by stepping up for a friend. The mom who is amazed at the transformation in her child.

You will find the stories of people who—just like at camp—you'd have never met and never known without this experience. The group of children who already have criminal records, learning that poetry might be a solution. The counselor who got a star named after her—in one family's sky—for taking the time to do what we all do each day at camp. The brave Palestinian and Israeli kids who risked societal rejection to build bridges with each other.

Furthermore, you will find your inspiration. Camp people, in the wise words of my dear friend Michael Brandwein, do hard things. When those hard things feel overwhelming, or even thankless, this book will serve as the constant reminder to you and any other staff person or camp parent you know that this is why kids need camp. This is why the world needs camp.

Only Michael Jacobus could have brought us these stories and crafted a larger one from the sum of their parts. Michael lives camp, in his days and in his heart.

Camp is Michael's profession. He's held more than 30 different staff positions at camps—often more than one at once. After all, why would his experience be different in that way from the rest of us, right? He visits camps all over the world. He trains countless staff people to be their best selves on the job. All of that is admirable, as well as life-changing.

More importantly, though, camp is Michael's calling. He sees the possibility in every staff member and in every camper, and he brings that spark to a flame. The mission of camp is to change lives, and that mission must be fed each camp day. The activities offered to children, the names of groups and bunks, and the view from the dining hall all serve as the setting for the true work. The true work is to reach a camper's soul and let them know that what you find there is perfect. In this book, Michael offers us the width and breadth of inspiration to keep doing that work day after day.

—Dr. Deborah Gilboa, MD
Parenting & Youth Development Expert
AskDoctorG.com

CONTENTS

INTRODUCTION

When I wrote my first book, *The Camp Director's Survival Guide*, I included a section of real-life stories from camp directors around the country. My goal was for camp directors to share some of the challenges they faced during their time at camp and the solutions that were eventually found. During these conversations, I heard such wonderful stories about how camp had changed their lives or the lives of their campers and staff, so many in fact that I decided to begin a separate project just for those stories.

When I speak at camp conferences, very often I will ask the assembled audience, "How many of you in this room, do what you do for the paycheck?"

No one ever raises their hand. That's because being a camp professional is not about the personal income. It's all about the OUTCOME!

When asking the camp community for stories for this book, all I had to do was ask another very simple question, "Why do you do what you do?" Many people found it difficult to pick just one story from a lifetime of camp adventures.

I then began receiving stories from all over the country; some were about campers, some were about staff, and some were about the camp directors themselves and how their lives had been forever changed by the camp experience. There was even some online blog content that I was fortunate enough to run across, and a few of those postings are included in this book as well.

I also learned that sharing conversations about life-changing, camp experiences was far easier than getting these very busy people to take the time and actually write it all down. When and if I ever do a project like this again, I may have to just take an audio recorder to a camp conference, invite camp pros to have a seat, and start talking.

My humble and heartfelt appreciation goes out to those individuals who took the time to share the stories shared in this book.

STORIES ABOUT CAMPERS

Secret Super Powers

Michael Jacobus

As I noted in my introduction, most every camp professional I know has that one (or quite often, more than one) story that cements into their being, that they are in the right place, the right job, and doing what most feeds their soul. For me, that story is about a young man named Mateo, who was just about to cross the line of physical degeneration from crutches to wheelchair, as he battled muscular dystrophy.

Mateo is my camper hero. Young Mateo was an eight-year-old camper attending a week-long resident camp program as a camper with the Muscular Dystrophy Association (MDA).

Every child attending the camp was afflicted with muscular dystrophy. Each camper was at different stages of the disease. Early-stage kids were pretty mobile, needing only some basic crutches and occasionally leg-braces. Mid-stage kids were in wheelchairs, while advance-stage kids were completely immobile and traveled in fully automated electric chairs, often with the need for head and next support.

The theme for the week was Super Heroes. As a result, all the camp counselors, personal aides, and staff were dressed in a colorful variety of Superman, Batman, and Wonder Woman outfits (including a few I've never seen before).

During the opening ceremony, campers were invited to select their own personal superpower. They were told that they could share the secret with their camp counselor, but not to tell anybody else. The underlying concept was that at the end of the week, during the closing campfire, everyone's secret superpowers would be revealed. At various times during the week, different things would happen that would allow the campers to try to guess each other's secret superpower, and they would write notes about each other and put them in a big box on the main stage.

Anticipating the arrival of this group, we had modified our zip line to the area several months earlier to accommodate limited mobility and wheelchair-bound campers. Thursday morning had been designated as the time that these kids would go up to the zip line. Accordingly, after breakfast everyone headed in that direction.

As you might imagine, it took up pretty much the whole day to get this group through the activity. Just the process of getting everyone into a safety harness took at least five times longer than usual.

When finally it was Mateo's turn, he worked his way up to the front of the line and onto the zip-launching platform. He would keep his leg braces on for his trip down the zip line but had to turn over his crutches to his camp facilitator.

Once the safety tether was attached to his harness, a very strange look came across his face. It's not unusual for kids, as well as adults, to feel fear right before going down the zip line. The look on Mateo's face was different, however. He looked concerned and worried.

His camp facilitator asked him if anything was wrong. Mateo responded:

"My secret super power is flying,
but now it won't be a secret anymore."

Relief, goose bumps, and a "down-to-our-soul" feeling that this moment was why we were involved in this particular situation, in this particular venue, came across everyone present. Even the volunteer firefighters who had come to help the kids that day started crying.

Mateo soared across the canyon, free (if only for a few seconds) from the gravity he had spent most of his young life fighting. He wore a smile on his face like no other, and all the assembled campers, staff, and volunteers cheered like he had scored the winning touchdown in the Super Bowl.

Not a dry eye could be found in the house. Everyone was filled with an extreme sense of purpose and clarity. In that moment, we were one—one family, one community, one super hero fan club.

First Ride

Cassie "Petri" Turner

My very first summer working at camp is a summer that I will never forget. I had just turned 18 years old and had no clue concerning what I was getting myself into. There were ups, and there were downs, as well as moments that I will remember for a lifetime.

One such moment came the morning of the last day of a session. The girls were all packed up and in the dining hall, enjoying there last meal together with their new friends and favorite staff. My job for the day was to "guard the parking lot" (aka, greet the parents and keep them from wandering the camp when they arrived early to pick up their daughters). One mom did just that.

She arrived just as the girls were headed into the dining hall. I approached her and greeted her with the usual, "you're early and will have to wait" spiel. She told me that she knew she would be early and didn't mind waiting, particularly if there was a place she could set up her camp chair to hang out in while she waited.

I invited her to hang out with me, if she was interested. After a little while, she returned from her car with a chair and magazine. While we waited, she started asking questions about camp. It was the usual small talk.

After a few minutes, she asked me what my favorite memory of the whole week was. I informed her that I was a wrangler (riding staff). As such, I had the opportunity to work with 48 different girls and teach them about horses and basics of riding. I then started to tell her of one girl in particular who had made my week.

She was a girl of about 11 or 12, with special needs, who was amazing to work with. I described to the mom my experience in working with the young girl and how wonderful it was to see her smiling and so happy. We were even able to get the young girl trotting with the other girls on their last day of riding. That was my favorite moment of the whole week.

When I was done telling my story to her, the mom then said she was thankful that I was there and was able to share a story about the young girl, who turned out to be her daughter, with her. In turn, I was also very happy that I was able to share that moment.

To this day, I may not remember the name of that young girl. I do, however, remember her smile and laugh at the exact moment that she first got her horse trotting, so very long ago. I also recall the mother being very excited when I was able to share a story about her daughter with her. While we may, on occasion, forget names, we never forget faces or those moments that we hold close to our hearts.

Finally

Becky Leary

I never thought, "Cancer camp is my favorite place to be," would be something that I would say to numerous friends, family members, classmates, and even strangers, on a regular basis. Nonetheless, that is what Camp Goodtimes has become for me—the most joy-filled and meaningful week of my year.

Camp Goodtimes is the pediatric oncology camp where I volunteer to help serve children who have had cancer, as well as their siblings, ages 7 through 17. My family was introduced to the camp when my younger sister was diagnosed with a brain tumor in 2003. A few years later, she was healthy enough to attend, and I went with her as a sibling for three wonderful years. At that point, I aged out and transitioned to a staff position.

A small group of volunteers plan year-round, finding donations and vendors, as well as 150 additional volunteers willing to donate 10 days of their summer toward helping restore some of the childhood experiences that are often lost by children and their siblings when one of the kids is battling cancer. The camp is a one-week energy-athon for its staff, jam-packed with special activities, such as a one-day cruise, a carnival, and a whipped-cream fight, in addition to normal camp activities, like archery, fishing, and arts and crafts.

A few years ago, we integrated an optional program for the campers who were siblings. Our main objectives were to bring them together, provide an opportunity to share their stories, and ask each other questions. Above all else, however, our goal was for them to be 100 percent surrounded by other children who have had a sibling with cancer.

Since that first year, the special sibling program has almost doubled in attendance. In the process, it has been an avenue for insightful and inspirational conversations between campers and staff about their sibling's and their own journeys. The sibling program has provided opportunities for sibs to speak openly, in a judgment-free zone, as well as bond with each other over their similar shared experiences.

One summer, while making the rounds to the cabins to extend a personal invitation to each sibling and explain what the program was all about, I had a particularly meaningful experience with a young camper. That year, I was a cabin counselor for a group of 11-year-old girls, one of whom was your classically adorable, bald, recently off-treatment, young lady who had a seven-year-old sister in our youngest girl's cabin. As I handed out invitations to the "littles," as we often refer to them, and gave the general explanation that we would be gathering to play some fun games, as well as share our stories, the younger sister of my camper let out a long-suppressed sigh and said to herself, "finally."

I was immediately taken back to all of the feelings of anger, fear, worry, resentment, guilt, and overwhelming confusion that I had had before, during, and after my sister was going through treatment. I felt deeply connected to this particular girl, before any of the carefully planned activities or discussions that were to follow, by her utterance of just one exhausted word, "finally."

Working with children for a number of years has brought me to the realization that close to 99 percent of what comes out of their mouths is meant to impress their peers or make them laugh. This comment, however, was involuntary and personal. It was akin to gasping when something has startled you, or bursting out in laughter before you can help it.

I was so taken aback by this little seven-year-old's reaction that it was hard for me to continue my routine speech. I remembered how I never had any opportunities like this to talk about my experience. I even felt a pang of jealousy. While no parent ever wants to neglect a child, having one in the hospital naturally takes up a lot of time and energy. As a result, the other sibling(s) often are left to face the ordeal virtually on their own. Having personally experienced being a sibling of a cancer patient, it was a very meaningful moment to bring a sense of comfort to one of our youngest siblings.

At camp, we strive to bring joy and silliness to the lives of those affected by cancer with some crazy activity, or by counselors wearing wacky costumes or just generally embarrassing themselves. In this moment, however, I saw us bring a wave of relief to a young girl, providing her with an opportunity to debrief a traumatic event in her life.

This story is a manifestation of why I work throughout the year and volunteer my time in the summer—to create moments for kids like that little girl to "finally" be able to comfortably share their experiences as a sibling of a cancer patient. Moments like this fuel my drive to not only bring camp to the kids with cancer, but to their siblings as well.

It Takes a Village
Kevin J. Costin

The first week of the first year that I was a camp director was for a camp called "Expressions: Talk Up Not Down," an entity that worked with at-risk teens. Most of the campers had already been arrested for a myriad of crimes. All of the staff who worked at the camp previously warned me how "bad" the campers were and that it was going to be extremely challenging. I was very nervous before the camp started, and had serious concerns about what I had gotten myself into.

The campers from this camp were all high school-age students who came from Washington D.C. Except for the campers who had been to the camp before, none of the campers had an exposure to nature or life outside the city. The camp itself was actually an expressions camp, where the campers were taught to employ poetry and art as a form of expression, rather than to use violence.

The camp had professional poets and artists, whose role was to work with the campers concerning how to express themselves. My staff and I were responsible for the other camp activities, such as hikes, games, team-building, and other fun activities that would help get their minds off of any disturbing issues that had been brought up in their poetry sessions. Subsequently, there were several moments during the eight-day camp when I realized that I was fulfilling my purpose in life.

Each day, we would take a nature walk and either just explore the outside or go over a specific topic about nature. During the nature walks, I would often hear screams. The screams resulted because of an encounter with a spider, some other kind of critter, or simply stepping into some mud. I often relish the sounds of screams during the nature hikes, not because I am a sadist and like to torture children, but rather the fact that I know I am exposing these kids to an environment in which they have never been and pushing their comfort levels in a safe and (somewhat) controlled environment.

Another fulfilling moment came when we were all walking to breakfast after the first night at camp. One of the first-time campers was walking with me and said, "last night was the first night in my life where I can remember not hearing gunshots while I was trying to sleep." I honestly didn't know how to respond to what I had just heard. I have grown up and lived in a rural community my whole life and hear gunshots from hunting all the time. I couldn't imagine these kids having to hear gunshots outside their homes on a nightly basis, trying to go to sleep, but also worrying about what's going on right outside their bedroom window.

The final moment that I would like to share occurred on the last night of the camp. This particular instance solidified my belief in the power of camp. On the last night of camp, everyone went to a performing arts center nearby, where the campers performed their poems on stage. During the performance, I heard several powerful and saddening stories—personal stories about abuse, drugs, homelessness, rape, and all the other evils of the world.

For me, the best part of the night wasn't about the poems themselves (although they were good and often brought me to tears). Rather, the best part of the night was after the performance, when everyone was mingling with the audience in the lobby. During this period, I got to see the campers socializing with family members, friends, and community leaders, all of whom were on hand to support the campers in changing their lives.

It was very heartwarming to see such encouragement and backing for these young people. It does, in fact, take a village to raise a child. It was quite fitting for the campers to know that they are not alone in this world. As such, there are people in the world who care about them—myself included.

Never Stop Moving Forward

Jenny Wilder

Our facility runs a special camp each year for military families. To qualify, families must have had one member become wounded, disabled, or fallen in the line of duty. The whole focus of the camp is geared toward the family moving past the terrible things that have happened to them and grow stronger together. On numerous occasions, a family's whole world is changed, because their loved one either never comes home or comes home a very different person than they were before serving.

This past summer, we had a mom with two kids, a boy and a girl. The dad was not at camp with them. The family dynamic was strained toward the beginning of the week. It was clear, however, that camp was helping them. Eventually, the kids started opening up.

On the last day of camp, the whole family came out to go on the zip-line. The mom did not want to go, but her son (whom we'll call Frank) did. He got up to the top of the net and completely froze.

Subsequently, Frank started crying hysterically and asked to be let down. I did my best to talk him through it and eventually got him attached to the zip-line. He started panicking again, so I sat down next to him in an effort to make him more comfortable.

By this point, his mom had figured out what was going on and got into position to talk to him on the ground. She started telling him to think about his father and do it for him. I didn't know what the relationship or status of Frank's father was.

In turn, I just told Frank to think about his dad and how proud he would be of him. Frank managed to get both hands on the zip-line for a split second before panicking again and taking them off (participants are required to have two hands on the zip-line for it to be safe). I told him that I hate going backwards in life. I also told him that I was proud of him because he had both hands on the zip-line. On the other hand, I reiterated my point that he should never go backwards in life. While he took a step in the right direction by putting both hands on the line, he needed to keep going that direction. Eventually, he got his courage up and went off the zip tower under his own power.

Later on that night, the families got the opportunity to write letters to anyone to whom they wanted. Some wrote to staff members, others wrote to their families, some just doodled. I was sitting in the back of the room watching them.

Subsequently, the mom came up to me holding a letter, tears streaming down her face. She went on to tell me that the kids' father was dying from kidney failure, and that she had gotten the call just before coming to camp that he was not going to last much longer. Because she did not want to upset the kids, she was waiting until camp ended to tell them.

She told me that she appreciated my working with Frank on the zip-line, particularly my message to him to never stop moving forward in life and keep going. Furthermore, she stated that they were about to be going into some hard times and that she appreciated the light that camp gave them.

After I finished talking to the mother, Frank came up to me with a letter of his own. He thanked me for helping him and said that he wanted to show me something. He took me outside and asked what I saw. When I told him that I saw stars, he said that his father and he always name stars for people who mean a lot to them. He pointed at the brightest star in the sky and told me that that was my star, because I was such a light in the world.

Camp changes lives. It might seem like it's just having fun and playing games, but what we do matters. In reality, the smallest things we do or say (like never going backwards) can have a huge impact on the people we serve. Camp staff should never ever forget this point when they're tired and hot, and it seems like the summer is never going to end.

Keith

Catherine Gorecki

Keith was the camper whom you secretly wished would wake up with the chicken pox and get sent home early. He was everywhere, mouthing off, terrorizing other boys, poking at the live animals with sticks, and leaving a trail of headaches and chaos in his wake. He stole tent poles that collapsed the tents while people were sleeping in them. He sank a canoe—on purpose. He got banned from the shooting ranges during the safety talk on the first day. He sent an entire group of first-year campers into a patch of poison sumac. He stole from the camp store, and refused to let grace be said without a burp or an outrageous comment. He knocked over young trees, and carved swear words into any surface he could find. Furthermore, he was in my session.

Subsequently, I tracked down Keith's troop leader to find out how I could get through to Keith. His answer came with a sigh. "Keith is here on scholarship. His home life isn't very good. He probably won't go back to school this year. Don't worry about teaching him anything. I don't think he'll be with the troop much longer."

Part of me was relieved. No one was expecting me to do wonders for Keith. Nobody cared what he did. Then, I got angry. Nobody cared what he did? As a consequence, I made Keith my new goal. I was going to care.

I found Keith at meals and free time, usually carving into a picnic table behind the dining hall with a butter knife. I sat near him, talked to him, and asked him about his day. Sometimes, he'd walk away or simply ignore me; other times, he'd explode, demanding to know why I wouldn't leave him alone. He was desperately trying to convince me to stop bothering him. In fact, there were days my stomach hurt at the thought of spending another afternoon in his withering presence.

My fellow camp counselors thought I was crazy. What difference could I possibly make? This kid was in need of professional help, not some tree-hugger, with a can-do attitude. They told me that I was wasting my time, that his leader obviously knew his situation better than I did, and that if he felt Keith was a lost cause, then I should let it go and focus on other things, like the Scouts who didn't leave me in tears.

I was determined to care about Keith. I ignored his insults and looked for something that he enjoyed. Eventually the insults stopped, and I learned how much he liked solving problems. I gave him jobs in the nature area, such as creating habitats, designing the layout of the greenhouse, and helping figure out how to prevent flooding on the trails.

Subsequently, at the end of the week he left—with a merit badge and a high-five. I felt I'd done my job well. In 12 hours, a new group of boys would be arriving at camp. As such, Keith slowly faded from my memory. On the other hand, my story about Keith doesn't end at this point.

Fast-forward 10 years, I was visiting my college alma mater, attending a lecture given by one of my favorite professors. As I was crossing the street, I heard somebody holler my name. I ignored it; surely, there was a student with the same name nearby. Hearing my old camp nickname, however, stopped me in my tracks. "CAT LADY GECKO! IF THAT'S YOU STOP WALKING!"

A young man ran over and threw his arms around me, wearing the biggest smile I'd ever seen and talking a mile a minute. He finally stepped back, and with the same emotion of every returning camper I'd ever met asked, "Do you remember me?" He must have seen the confusion on my face. He went on to exclaim, "It's me! Keith! From Lost Lake! You helped me get a merit badge!" It all came crashing back to me—Keith!

We decided to go to the student center for coffee. I learned that after he earned his badge at camp, he told his science teacher about what he had accomplished that summer. The teacher helped him connect his passion to his studies. He graduated from college—the first to do so in his family. As he was walking me to my car, he told me, "You know, I'm here on scholarship. I'm going to be an engineer. I'm going to make things better. Just like you taught me. Just like at camp."

I cried in my car that night—not because Keith had succeeded, but because his success didn't depend on a merit badge or a grade or a class. It depended on the people who refused to let him give up on himself, the individuals who made it a point to care. People like his science teacher, and individuals like me. In reality, sitting down at that picnic table one afternoon changed everything.

Boys to Men

Lisa Merlotti

One summer, I was working at scout camp. We had a boy who had cerebral palsy and was wheelchair-bound. Since I was in the nature area and most badges were within his physical reach, he got stuck in our area most of the time. As the week progressed, his dad would go with us as we went off-roading with his chair. We did bird study off-trail and event plant study.

On the Wednesday of that week, I went to my post on the Honor Trail (a mile-long hike up a mountain with four stops, in which you listen to one of four Baden Powell letters). This trek was a quiet and reverent hike and one of my favorite aspects of camp. Furthermore, it was a small footpath up a true mountain in the Yellowstone wilderness, which his chair would surely not be able to transverse. I sighed as I saw his group coming, knowing he would not be able to successfully complete this activity. As the group shuffled up to my station, there he stood, held up on each arm by two scoutmasters. Subsequently, they sat him down on the adjacent camp stool and paused to hear me recite my Baden Powell letter.

I could barely get the words out, as I realized how special this moment was, not only for him, but all of us as well. As the group stood to leave, the unthinkable happened; two 13-year-old boys pushed their scoutmasters aside, and took the arms of their friend to walk him up the mountain. In that moment, I knew that this was what camp was about. Young boys were being shaped into young men, right before my eyes.

Later that week at closing campfire, this boy's father gave me a hug and thanked me for introducing him and his son to a new hobby. They had fallen in love with birdwatching, which would be their new activity together. Camp is not only about impacting the lives of children while they are at camp, but also changing them for the better after they leave.

Enter Carson

Fabio Del Carlo

Carson was my camper for five consecutive years, at a seven-week residential summer camp in the New York Catskills.

As "camp people," most of us have experienced or dealt with homesickness. I've always enjoyed exchanging stories with friends and camp pros on the topic, sharing from our own wild experiences. Most of these stories end up with either the camper getting over it and enjoying the rest of camp, or going home. My story is a bit different, not only because it lasted five years, but because it changed my life.

I was incredibly excited when I got an offer for my first sleep-away camp job. Having just finished my second year of college, I couldn't wait to get to camp. Upon arrival at camp, I felt quite overwhelmed, initially during staff training, meeting so many new people, as well as finding out more information about my campers.

I had no prior camp experience, so this was all fairly new to me. Something clicked, however, after we got "Ditterized" at one of Bob Ditter's training sessions. Here I was, opening day, ready to meet my campers, full of confidence, and everything planned out in my head.

We head out to the buses with my beautiful "BUNK 1" sign that I had made myself to welcome our campers. We walk the boys to the bunk, and it's going great! We're all talking, unpacking, getting to know each other, and then suddenly (as if time stood still), "ENTER CARSON."

Carson, then eight years old, was a first-year camper—an athletic, popular kid. He was already familiar with some of the boys in the bunk, through family friends. He also had two cousins who were campers in older divisions, and a sister who was a second-year teen camper. What a great thing to come to a camp with your favorite cousins, your big sis, and some friends right? Not quite. From the very first night, while other boys played some bunk basketball or played cards, Carson laid in his bed and stuffed his face on his pillow, an image I would experience many more times.

The first two nights, Carson didn't really respond to anyone, or talk to counselors at all. He would just lay in his bed and cry. Then, one morning, just before our first activity the yelling begins. "I WANNA GO HOME!" he would shout, "I HATE IT HERE!" On day three, Carson was admitted into the infirmary. In one sense, we'd like to say he was so homesick, he actually got sick. On the other hand, we'll go with a mild fever.

I was not prepared for this situation. I had everything planned out in my head about how the summer was going to be, making great relationships with my campers and going above and beyond to be the "best counselor!" The first week really threw me off.

Other counselors stopped by the infirmary to see how Carson was doing, while I worked on my secret master plan to find a "cure for homesickness." My co-counselors said things like, he was "getting worse," he was "flippin out," he "kicked a nurse." Eventually, I finally decided to go see him after dinner. Although I spent all day trying to think about what to say to him, or what I could do to help, I still had no idea.

Subsequently, I made my way into the infirmary, where he's lying in a bed, with both his hands covering his eyes, crying, and breathing heavily. "Hi, Carson" I said. The only response I ever got included several grunts and sounds of extreme agony. At one point, he started tossing and turning violently, yelling, and hitting the wall. I remained calm, and kept trying to speak to him.

Just as I was about to give up and go back to the bunk, a few things that Bob Ditter talked about popped into my head. Specifically, the part about homesickness and his famous "money in the bank" talk. I began to talk to Carson about home. "What do you miss about home?" I asked. It was the first time I got an answer that night, "My mom, my dad, my Labradoodle."

We talked about them, and he told me everything about his mom, his dad, his family, dog, school, and so on. In turn, I told him about my family, and how I haven't seen my dad in a long time, and I'm missing him too. For the first time, I felt like we were able to relate and understand each other.

We talked for about two hours. Carson had calmed down, and even smiled a few times. There was something special happening in this situation. I was getting ready to leave, when Carson quickly grabbed my hand and said, "Please stay, I don't want to be alone." As a result, I got permission from my division leader and spent the night at one of the infirmary beds, we put on a VHS video of the "Stuart Little" movie, and that was it. That night I felt like I had made huge progress with Carson, and maybe this homesickness thing would soon be a thing of the past.

Well … I WAS WRONG. In fact, Carson was "homesick" for the weeks that followed as well—in fact, until the very last day of camp. His parents absolutely did not want him to come home. In their minds, he had to "get through this." In reality, five years later, he was still "getting through it."

When visiting days came along, it did not make things any better. Carson is known for his famous visiting day tantrums. We joke around and say he "plans his escape" every summer. The first year, when one of the counselors had to hold him down as his parents left, Carson bit him in the arm. His second year, when his cousin had to keep him in the bunk, Carson kicked him in the junk, and then attempted to make a run for it. The list goes on … and on.

Every year Carson returned to camp, I'd hope that he would be different. For four years, however, there wasn't much change. Year four was perhaps the worse year for Carson, because he had broken his arm and had to wear a cast for most of the summer. He would often sneak out to his cousins' bunks, and refused to participate in any activities. He would sit in his bed crying, and demand to call home to speak to his parents.

One day, Carson decided to make a run for the front gates. He started sprinting toward the bridge, and I went after him. As I approached the bridge, he made a sudden stop and threw a huge rock right at me. Somehow, after sprinting for half a mile, I was able to do a spin move and dodge out of the way of the rock, which just missed my head. Eventually, I caught up with him and took him down … gently. This was it; after four years, I came to the realization that maybe this camp wasn't for Carson, maybe it would be best if he went home.

I never disliked Carson. He was a nice kid. Ever since that night in the infirmary, I was the person to whom he would always come talk. He trusted me and felt comfortable talking to me. As a result, we had a very special connection. I can't remember how many times in the last five summers, Carson and I have sat outside on the porch and just talked. Sometimes, we wouldn't even talk. There would just be silence, but he wanted to sit out there with me. We still talked about home, about camp, and about the things he missed from home. Somehow, Carson was able to get through each summer.

Year five started out much like every other "Carson summer." It was my first year as a division leader, and out of the bunk. It was different for me, and different for the boys as well, with brand new counselors for the first time. This time Carson only felt homesick for the first two weeks.

We kept talking, almost every night out on the porch. By now, it was like a tradition. One night, out of nowhere, Carson asked, "How's your dad?" "What?" I said, very confused. "Your dad, the one you haven't seen, that you told me about that time." This circumstance was one of the most memorable moments of my camp career. Carson remembered the conversation that we had five years ago about missing our dads.

I explained to Carson that I still hadn't talked to my dad. Then, Carson said, "You should call him, he's your dad." Trying to hold back tears that night, everything suddenly made sense to me: I realized how much of an impact that we can have on a child's life at camp. Most importantly, however, I came to understand how much they can impact our lives.

After that summer, I decided to call and reconnect with my dad. As such, I'm very happy to have him back in my life. I am also thankful for my "pain-in-the-neck" camper for motivating me to take that step, and for making my five years at camp the best years of my life.

Super Fly Seniors

Stuart Jones

Andrew was a 14-year-old 9th-grader, attending camp for the first time. His father had a severe stroke prior to camp and was on long-term disability. His mother was working full-time and caretaking the entire family. Andrew, who had experienced a rough, mostly unsuccessful 8th-grade year, started camp visibly "skeptical" of everything we were offering and all that we thought we were about.

The night before Andrew's last day of camp, his mother sent us the following email:

> Well, the past three weeks have exceeded all of my hopes and expectations for our son. I already knew that it would be exactly what Andrew needed. He was reluctant to admit that he was enjoying it and having fun, and yet every night, he had story upon story to relate to us. We had to sneak up on it, because if I asked directly, I received a lukewarm response like, "Camp's okay." On the other hand, But if I just allowed the space for the talk to emerge naturally, it all came out.

Tonight, when we were at the grocery store, he got sad. I could see it in his face. I said, "I know what you're thinking. You're missing your friends from camp, aren't you?" He gave me the "how-does-my-mom-know-everything?" look and then gave me a huge hug.

We had made an almost nightly ritual of going to the store, so he could get his sandwich for the next day. He loved getting treats to share with his friends. He is a very generous, giving soul. and loves to bring things for people. I could have easily made a sandwich for him every night, but he loved this time that was just with me … going to the store, while dad was at home. In fact, Andrew and I had some special times together.

A relatively simple, but very profound, message from a loving mother.

So, tonight, when we walked in the same grocery store that we had been going to almost every weeknight for the past three weeks, I know that he felt the twinge of "I don't have camp tomorrow. It's over. I want to see my friends again." As we walked by the freezer section, one pane of glass was frosted over. Andrew walked up to it and wrote Super Fly Seniors (his group's name). It brought tears to my eyes. He felt so connected.

I wanted to start by painting the picture for you of what I have seen in my son thanks to you and what you've created. People like you who create gorgeous experiences for children are the kind of people I feel honored to meet and know. You have done something amazing. Thank you.

That's a story that reminds us we're in the right business.

A Tale of Two Camps and Two Campers

James Ferrigan

I was the program director for a number of Cub camps over the years. One particular Cub/parent team of campers stands out in my memory, which I will refer to as Mom and Matt. While they both arrived at the same facility, they attended two different camps.

Mom and Matt arrived late on a summer's Sunday afternoon by themselves. The other campers from their Pack had already been processed and were setting up their camp. Mom did not read the council-provided instructions about check-in, parking, and camp set-up.

When they initially arrived at camp, Mom tried to drive directly, if unsuccessfully, around the lake to a campsite. This situation prompted a radio call to camp HQ by one of the staffers, which is how I first met Mom and Matt. Mom was a single parent and raising Matt, a Bear Cub Scout (7- to 9-year-olds) by herself. She was caring enough to take the time to attend camp with her son, but she arrived with a host of expectations.

Taking over from my staffer, I intervened and explained to her that no cars were allowed at the campsites. As such, I directed them to the designated parking area. Mom immediately claimed that no one had told her that (the first hint that she had not read the parent guide). She then wanted to know about their gear, and how it would get to their campsite, and what about her car? I explained that because of her late arrival, the staffers who had been available to help were now otherwise engaged with other duties. On the other hand, we would try to accommodate her, and I called for the commissioner to meet us in the parking lot with the camp truck.

While I waited, Matt excitedly asked an endless series of questions. Where was the lake? When was swimming? Could he shoot BB guns? What about knives? When was dinner?

Mom, on the other hand, kept asking, "What was taking so long?" When the camp truck finally arrived, I asked her about her gear, and she indicated that it was all in the trunk. When she popped the lid, all we could see was Walmart bags. It appeared that she had stopped there on her way to camp. I queried her about her previous camping experience, to which she replied, "We do not camp that often." (Insert ever!)

We (Matt, the commissioner, and I) began to transfer their gear and suitcases, while Mom sat in the camp truck. As we drove around the lake, Matt continued his queries, "How cold was it? How deep was it? Mom asked, "How much farther to our campsite?"

Mom and Matt had been assigned to the far side of Blue Lake (a thermal-spring fed pond) in a scenic campsite among the trees next to the shoreline. The camp access road was up a trail on a slight bluff above the camp. We (the same three individuals) unloaded the car. At that point, Mom asked, "Who was going to set up camp?" Matt volunteered that he would.

We emptied the Walmart bags to discover a roomy pop-up tent with an ample awning large enough for Mom to stand upright in, camp cots, a cooler, sleeping bags, camp chairs, a camp table, flashlights, a lantern, and other camp ephemera, all designed to provide the comforts of home. Mom directed our efforts, including the placement of the tent and chairs so that she and her son could enjoy a view of the lake. I helped her get connected to the other adults from her Pack, whom she had yet to meet. She asked me where she could buy cigarettes, wine, cheese, and ice. (This was a second hint about her unfamiliarity with the leader guide.)

I explained about Scout camps and our camp policy regarding tobacco, alcohol, and food in the campsites. (Her third strike!) We got her squared away with her unit, and introduced Matt to his buddy, who promptly went off to sign up for his "Official BSA Whittling Chip," the wallet card that demonstrated his participation in a knife safety class, and the right to carry a pocket knife at camp. Mom, now in a bit of a huff, plopped down in one of her new Walmart chairs. I bid her adieu and returned to the main camp. I next encountered Mom and Matt at dinner. Matt had befriended other Cubs. Mom was complaining that the dining facility was picnic tables al fresco.

You can pretty much guess the rest. Mom was a fixture in main camp, with a litany of negative observations about our camp. There is too much dust. The trails were too rough. The activity areas were too far away from her campsite. She was appalled with our common showers. The Kybo (porta-potty) smelled. Her car was too far away. There was no laundry, infinitum ad nauseum.

Matt, on the other hand, was a blur. I saw him at the waterfront, where he qualified as a swimmer. I saw him in handicrafts, gleefully hammering out a bowl. I watched him thwack pie tins with kibble with a wrist-rocket and whack the other Bear Cubs with foam "swords." I saw him try and get a bull's-eye at the BB range. His Pack sang at the campfire. He took a nature hike. Not surprisingly, Matt slept well through his three nights at camp.

On the day of departure, Mom buttonholed me after breakfast insisting that she had to leave early. I got the commissioners to help her break camp and retrieved Matt's advancement records for him, as well as his camp patch. I gave Mom an evaluation form and agreed to meet them at their car.

When the camp truck brought them to the parking lot, Mom had one last complaint about how dirty her car had gotten while parked at our camp. She handed me her scathing evaluation form. She liked nothing about camp, and in the comments section, she'd scrawled, "I will never come here again!"

We loaded up their gear. It was time to say good-bye. I thanked them for coming and wished them Godspeed. Matt turned back to me, outstretched his arms, and gave me a mini-Smokey Bear hug and told me, "Thanks Jim, this was the best time I ever had." They then left.

I will always wonder about, and never know, is Matt's future dynamic? Did he go on in Scouting? I hope so, but at least he had one great camp experience. We did our job for him. I don't know if we ever could have pleased Mom. Mom came to camp with a predetermined set of expectations. From her, I learned that parent expectations are often just resentments under construction.

Matt, on the other hand, came to camp ready to suspend his disbelief and accept wonderment, that special wonderment of youth. For Matt, camp was not a "fail safe space," but rather a "space where he could fail safely," learn, and move on. This he did.

Thus, we have the Tale of Two Camps—two campers at the same time, same place, and experiencing two totally different camps.

Crossing the Invisible Boundary

Lupine Reppert

It was a camp like no other, striving to do a seemingly impossible thing—bring Palestinian, Israeli, and American youth together for dialogue, fellowship, and community. Many of the Middle East participants had never spoken to "the other," let alone slept in a cabin with them, broke bread with them, or trusted them with the intimate experience of telling their story. That's what we did with these brave young people, however. We all came to camp wanting something better—for the Middle East and for the world. Yet, the path to peace is not a clearly forged road. Rather, it is a backcountry trail, rarely maintained and full of twists and turns, overgrown weeds, and drop-offs.

My year as a counselor was an extremely difficult summer for our staff team. We were operating with the backdrop of a year that had been exceptionally violent in the Middle East. A number of our staff had lost someone that year due to the conflict. Furthermore, every Palestinian had been the victim of increased discrimination and oppression. Even though we were skilled in leading campers through dialogue exercises to build mutual understanding, we were struggling to stay connected to each other in a way that maintains trust. These issues finally flared up one evening at a staff meeting in the middle of the session. I will never forget that night.

We sat there in front of the campfire—Palestinians on one side, Israelis on the other in the dead of the night, trying to reconcile with each other the pain and hurt of the past 100 years. It was all there. These problems seemed to be insurmountable, with each individual's experience tangled up among one another—each holding truth and contradiction.

We talked and talked and talked, only to find these wounds even more open and exposed. Resentment among the groups was growing. We were becoming "the other" to one another once again, instead of the individual people that we had worked so hard to recognize in each other. What was to be done? We were caught in the maze of this conflict, always running into dead ends. It seemed the maze had no exit.

Eventually, we all reverted to silence, exhausted. Violet hadn't said much that night. She mostly just listened—which was typical for her. She was the individual who was usually quiet, but when she did speak up, it meant something. This time she didn't speak.

Violet stood up and crossed the invisible boundary of the campfire and hugged Tibah, a Palestinian, with all her might. She turned and crossed the boundary to hug Keren, an Israeli, and hugged her with all her might. Then, she crossed the boundary and hugged Farah with all her might. Next, she crossed the boundary and hugged Naomi with all her might. Violet hugged every person around the campfire. At that point, all together we got up and went to bed.

In the morning, we ate breakfast with our campers alongside each other. We then went on hikes, splashed in the pool alongside each other, and we sang each other's native songs. We finished a great camp session together, and created an experience together that these young adults would never forget.

Is this a happy ending? I'm not sure, but it's the truth. The reality of the situation is that solutions for the world's most difficult problems are not solved in one camp session or tied up in 500 words. Change comes from patient diligence and relentless hope. It comes from courageous conversations around the campfire, from eating side by side in the dining hall, and from singing each other's songs together.

It comes from giving hugs with all your might.

What Happens After Camp?

Danny Sudman

KINARD CARES is a student group from Kinard Middle School in Fort Collins, CO. These students are leaders in their school community and visit Catalina Island annually for a weeklong session at camp to bond, participate in service learning projects, and learn from lessons in the marine and terrestrial communities of Catalina Island. They return to their school with the resources and critical thinking skills to address social and environmental issues. Because I work with youth and adults in a safe and positive environment as a camp professional, the positive growth that occurs in these individuals is no surprise. What I don't often see, however, is how the camp experience translates beyond the camp environment.

The founder of this group and their trip leader, Chris Bergman, is a passionate educator who wanted to provide his students a unique learning opportunity to encourage leadership development. For three consecutive years during one week in the fall, I had the pleasure of facilitating this group through their camp experience. Each day, I was very excited as I watched the dynamic of the group develop as they worked together to complete the challenge course, work on ecological restoration projects, and learn about sustainability by exploring the rich natural communities of Catalina Island.

At the end of the week, I said goodbye to the KINARD CARES group as they headed home to Colorado. Over the short week, a strong rapport had been built amongst the teachers, students, and instructors. It was clear that their experiences at camp would carry on with them long after they returned home. During our closing, the students shared and reflected on the time that we had all spent together and what it meant to them. There were statements about the changes they would implement to make their school more sustainable, ways they could influence their community to address issues about which they were passionate and how they could be better students, children, friends, and neighbors.

Last year, I had the opportunity to see firsthand the results of the camp experience when I was invited to Kinard Middle School to speak with a group of students from the KINARD CARES program and tour their school. It felt like there was a role reversal; I was going to camp, and the campers would now be my counselors.

As I walked into the classroom, I was immediately greeted by some of the students in the group that had previously traveled to Catalina, when I was their instructor. We reminisced about our service learning projects and how others had followed in their footsteps to continue where their work had left off. One student in particular shared how her time within my group had influenced her decision to go to college to engage in environmental studies. I was thrilled to see that so many years later, my work as a camp professional continues to resonate through the youth with whom I have worked.

After speaking with the group about my work as a camp professional and the impact it's had on me, I was taken on a tour of the school. Ordinarily, when you take a tour, it's led by a school administrator. I was pleasantly surprised, however, when we began the tour, that a group of students began with an introduction of the mission and goals of Kinard Middle School, an award-winning blue and green ribbon school. We made our way through the school, stopping along the way to hear from each of the students about the educational and environmental practices of their school. As we entered the dining hall, I saw dozens of familiar signs hanging up in the area where food and trash are disposed. These signs were familiar to me, because they were recreated in the image of the signs used at our camp to show visitors how to compost and properly dispose of waste.

It's not fair to say that their time at camp is responsible for all aspects of their leadership abilities and the contributions they will go on to have in our society. After this experience, however, I think it's clear that camp definitely had an influence on these students. As leaders in their school community, these students continue to affect positive social and environmental change in their school, much of which was inspired by lessons learned at camp.

The Four-Year Climb

Cheryl Oliveria

While working at a day camp as the adventure coordinator, my role involved supervising the staff and programing on the high and low ropes course. I was employed at this camp for four years. This camp operated in conjunction with a local school that sent children with mild spectrum disorders to our camp, along with their own one-to-one campers.

Over the course of my four years at the camp, there was this one particular child who struggled with the idea of climbing the pole to get to the highest element. The first two years, he struggled to get off the ladder. By the third year, he made it on to the pole and off the ladder.

My fourth year at camp, this child succeeded everyone's expectations. It was a very sunny day, and he was determined. He showed absolutely no fear at all as he climbed the ladder. He slowly made his way up the telephone pole to the first landing. Once on the landing, I truly thought he would choose to come down, not because I didn't believe in him, but his past experiences indicated that he would probably do so.

When he stepped onto his the lily pad, everyone cheered with excitement! It was remarkable to see his face light up with joy and with just a twinge of fear. Well that day, he made it across all four of the lily pads to the end! His endeavor across the entire element took nearly an hour. No one cared. It was an amazing day, and he was thrilled to say that he had completed it.

MDA Summer Camp

Staci Lane

MDA Summer Camp offers a fun and safe outdoor experience, along with opportunities to engage in a variety of activities, such as adaptive sports, arts and crafts, camp dances, and much more. In addition to all of the fun and friendship it offers, MDA Summer Camp enables campers to stretch their comfort zones and grow in independence, as they spend a week away from home and permit someone other than their parents to provide personal care. While there's an abundance of fun and games at camp, if you talk to MDA campers, they'll tell you that the real benefits come in a much subtler form—the lifelong friendships, the increased self-esteem and confidence, and the chance to spend at least one week of the year in a place where physical disabilities are the norm, rather than the exception.

For parents and guardians, MDA camp provides a brief break from their roles of caregiver for a child with neuromuscular disease. It's a place where parents know they can send their children for a week of summer fun and, at the same time, be assured that their child's medical and physical needs will be met by a team of dedicated health professionals and trained camp volunteers. MDA staff and volunteers assume all camper care, including physical and emotional support, which allows parents much-needed time to attend to their own needs and, in some cases, spend some special time with the camper's siblings.

I've been a camp director with MDA since 2008 and have seen what a benefit this camp is for both the campers, as well as the parents. I have one story in particular that I'd like to share with everyone, a story that really touches my heart. Being a mom, I know how difficult it can be to let your kids go somewhere new.

We had a new camper, who was eight years old, join us at camp this past year. We had paired this young male camper with a female counselor, who was ready to go for the week. As mom arrived at camp with her son to check him in, our counselor joined mom and camper and spent the next three hours getting to know them. Throughout these hours, it was very apparent that the camper was not intending to let mom out of his sight, nor was he planning to let her leave him at camp. In this instance, we had a little guy who had never been away from home and didn't know anyone at camp. He was not planning to stay!

As dinner was approaching and parents were leaving, this mom had a decision to make. The counselor had already gone off to join another group, given that she was under the impression that her camper wasn't going to be staying at camp. Mom made a decision, that wasn't easy on any of us, but in the end it was the best decision she could have made. The evening was approaching, mom asked me to hold onto her son as she walked away.

The camper, at this point, came to realize what was happening. As he was kicking and screaming and swinging his fist to my face, my eye glasses went flying. I gently told the camper that he shouldn't hit me. He then started to calm down.

He saw his counselor walking up a hill with a group of others, and he instantly wanted to be with her. To him, she had already become a familiar face and someone he could trust. We called for her together, and she came to his side. Subsequently, he walked away with her. He had a blast the entire week of camp, and not once did he struggle with homesickness.

It brings tears to my eyes, because I can relate to this mom. In reality, I have experienced similar situations with my own children. I later talked with the mom, and she said that at one point she turned around, saw her son swinging at me, and almost came back to get him. She realized, however, that the opportunity for her son to be at our camp would help give him the social skills that he would need someday in order to live a life independent from her. This situation reveals why our MDA camp is so important for these kids and parents. Personally, I feel very honored to have the ability to help direct these camps each year.

Julia

Sergio Medrano

At the time, Julia was a second grader and an amazing and brave little girl. Not only was this Julia's first time away at camp, it was also her first time away from family and home.

A few months earlier, I was at Julia's school, promoting our camp program. Julia's parents were part of the audience. After the presentation, they had asked to speak with me in private. They shared with me their concerns about Julia being away from home for the first time. They were both equally as nervous. They were also excited for Julia and for the amazing experiences they both knew she would have—very much the same way they both did over several summers as youngsters. Did I mention that Julia's parents met at a similar camp for the first time when they were just kids themselves?

Julia didn't seem too concerned about our conversation. As a matter of fact, I was pretty sure that she wasn't even aware about her parents' plans for her to attend summer camp for a whole week. Julia's parents were both convinced that our camp program was a perfect match. I'd strongly suggested to them to have a lengthy conversation with her about camp to clearly explain what it meant to be away at camp by herself. They agreed, and I asked them to give me a call to share with me what their decision for Julia was … go, or not go.

Sunday morning, the designated pick-up site for camp came along quickly. Julia was waiting there, along with the other campers, and she looked as excited to be there as the rest of the kids. She was well prepped with all of her gear in hand. I spoke with Julia before checking her in, and yes, I was convinced that Julia was ready. She explained all of the different plans she had in mind once she made it to camp. I then gave the okay, and she boarded the bus with the rest of the kids, and they were on their way.

That same Sunday in the early afternoon, after a few hours on the road, the kids had arrived at our campsite. The energy around camp was electrifying, lots of activity and noise and excitement, a sort of controlled chaos. We sent the kids off to their cabins to familiarize themselves with their new living quarters, new friends, and counselor. All was great, and Julia was still fine. Dinner came along, and Julia was still doing okay. A quick calming activity after dinner for all of the groups, then bunk time, and finally, lights out.

The next day, on Monday morning, all of the campers showed up on time for breakfast, including Julia, with one "minor" change. During the night, right before lights out, things did not go so well for her. Pat, her counselor, informed me that Julia cried for most of the night. She even kept some of the other kids up. She was crying and crying, with no one able to console her. Some of the other counselors tried to help, but it didn't work.

Subsequently, Julia and I spoke for a few minutes during breakfast. After calming her down just enough, we both decided and agreed to wait until I called her parents and to give them until the end of day to get there. I told Julia that it was a long drive up the mountain. Reluctantly, Julia agreed and joined her group and had the opportunity to experience some of the planned morning activities. The idea was to expose Julia to some of the fun, with the hope that she would change her mind after spending some time with her group. I really wanted her to decide to stay the rest of the week.

Later, when Julia returned with her group for lunch, Pat, her counselor, reported that she was okay during the activities and, at times, was enjoying herself. As soon as she spotted me, she asked me, "Did you call my mom?" I told her that I did and that's when I had to break the bad news to her. "When are my parents coming to pick me up?" she asked. I told her that her parents were having trouble coming up because their car had broken down, and they didn't have a way to get to camp.

That's all it took. Julia was upset and began to cry again. I tried to console her and told her that her parents were trying to borrow a car from her grandma. That helped a little. Subsequently, Pat and I convinced her to stay with the group and participate in the next set of activities.

This whole thing about her parents and their car troubles went on for the better part of the week. Julia was literally stuck in camp. Julia's parents weren't going to be able to get to her until Friday, the LAST DAY of camp! Julia was still crying, but with less and less frequency, as the days passed. She made it past Tuesday to Wednesday and was doing better by then—still crying, but better. Thursday was pretty much the same, still crying, but less and less. She spent the day Thursday also willing to join in and participate a bit more with the others in her group. We had our last campfire scheduled for that Thursday night, right before going to bed. I was surprised that Julia was actually doing better during most of the day and into the night. This little girl impressed me. I couldn't have imagined the stress and angst that she might have felt the entire week.

Our last campfire was magical. A final bonding that would be felt and remembered by all participants for a long time to come, including Julia. During the last few minutes of campfire before dismissing everyone, I reminded them that it was our last night together and that we would be leaving the following morning.

I noticed through the crowd of campers as they were leaving that Julia had started to cry again, with no apparent end. I then glanced over at Pat and asked, "What now?" Pat shook her head and shrugged her shoulders to indicate that she had no idea.

I asked Julia and Pat to stay behind for a few minutes longer. I wanted to see if I could do something to try and make Julia feel better. I reminded her several times, "Julia, your mommy and daddy will be here tomorrow, everything will be better soon, I promise."

She gathered herself enough to put a few words together, "I-I-I know, I-I-I'm not crying because of that," she informed me. I was a bit confused, so I asked her, "Then, why are you crying?" Trying to compose herself, she said, "I-I-I'm crying cuz i-i-it's over."

Still confused, I asked her again, "Why?" She repeated, "I-I-I'm crying cuz i-i-it's over. I won't get to see my new friends and my new family again!"

At the end of the day, Julia simply didn't want to leave. The magic of camp!

Lighting the Way
Lani Connolly

As a pre-teen, Jessica's life took a sudden turn. Her mother died from ovarian cancer. The disease came on suddenly, the struggle was brief and violent, and before anyone could get their minds and hearts around what was happening, Jessica's mother was gone. Jessica's world went into a tailspin. Her home life was disrupted. Her grades tumbled, and she started spending a good deal of time alone. At 14, Jessica found herself doubting everything, including herself.

It was that summer, that Jessica was offered a campership to Teaming for Tomorrow. This residential camp program is intended to give adolescent girls a vision for the future and equip them with practical life skills to help them realize the futures they envision. The first evening of camp, the girls have a chance to sign up for the workshops that interest them.

While other campers chatted excitedly amongst themselves about what they wanted to do in the week ahead, I noticed that Jessica's voice was silent. Standing toward the back of the room, Jessica radiated loneliness and uncertainty. She hadn't put her name down for a single workshop.

I didn't fully understand the circumstances of Jessica's life then, but it was clear that Jessica would need extra encouragement and safe space in order to bloom. The camp staff and I set to work. I approached her, introducing myself and asking her a series of get-to-know-you questions. When asked, "What is it that you like to do?" Jessica's answer was, "I dunno—I'm just not good at anything." Despite this response, something about Jessica suggested that buried beneath that quiet demeanor was a deep thinker, with a great deal of natural curiosity. Working together, we charted a course of activities for her camp week that included exploring the field of engineering through a series of hands-on workshops. She moaned, but agreed to give it a try.

The turning point for Jessica came in the flashlight-building workshop. In order to build flashlights, the girls would have to solder the connections themselves. Many girls were hesitant, including Jessica. "Don't leave me," she said. "I can't do this." But, she did. In fact, she was one of the best in the group.

With each successful solder joint, Jessica's confidence grew. The other individuals in the group took note, and began asking Jessica for help. By the time the workshop was over, Jessica had a working flashlight and a host of new friends. Jessica's smile could not be contained. She emerged from that workshop invigorated. She embraced the challenge of every workshop to follow, quickly building a following among the other campers, who recognized and validated her ability.

Jessica still keeps in touch. She has done well, building upon the interest and self-efficacy that was sparked that summer. At age 15, Jessica founded a robotics team that competes annually in the FIRST Tech Challenge—advancing to even new worlds for her. Passionate about instilling confidence in other youth, she has created science and math programming for her local library, and has earned her Girl Scout Gold Award for leadership and service.

Jessica credits that camp experience with instilling a sense of empowerment in her. She reinforced my immense satisfaction in the impact that her camp experience had on her, when she stated to me, "You told me to set my sights high, that I can accomplish anything, and when I replied that I don't think I can do this, you said 'think again!'" For the record, Jessica will enter college this fall as a mechanical engineering major.

STORIES ABOUT CAMP STAFF

Eternally-Effervescent Development

TJ Roberts

I stepped away from the camp environment to get my masters in recreation administration in 2011, with the full intention of returning upon graduation, but other opportunities and life adventures took me down another path. I was asked to teach at the undergraduate level and develop a health and wellness program for a small private college immediately after I graduated with both my MS and personal training certificate. Once the program was established, I wanted to take the jump and try running my own personal training business, which brings me to the present day.

The reason I share this story is because these last five years of my life would never have happened had it not been for my years dedicated to the camp environment. I spent 2007-2011 engulfed in camp culture serving year-round in roles for outdoor education, summer camp (both residential and day camps), and conference retreat programming. Most people say that you will learn the most about yourself during the four or five years you spend away at college. Rest assured, however, I learned more about myself during the years at camp.

The camp environment nourishes each individual who steps foot into its sphere of influence. There is an organic truth that tends to guide each experience at camp which, I believe, can be summed up as "eternally-effervescent development." I use the word effervescent to describe the vivacious, youthful atmosphere found in a camp setting. The development never ceases for camp individuals. From the campers to the camp professionals, the maintenance crew to the kitchen staff, everyone seems to continually develop their multiple intelligences, as Howard Gardner would describe it.

Camp gives participants the opportunity to explore new talents, learn new skills, and interact with others in a way that will challenge thinking, but also foster empathy toward other individuals from different backgrounds, thanks to the care and guidance of the professionals involved. The professionals are challenged to adapt rapidly to keep up with the feverish pace associated with childcare, as well as maintaining professionalism within a high-stress, high-reward, work environment.

No one can predict the future, but talk exists that our public schools are currently failing both our youth and its teachers. Thus, they are failing our future generations. Perhaps the public school system will start to adapt by taking some lessons out of the camp playbook to help right some of the wrongs mentioned in that conversation among school professionals … but I digress.

On the other hand, I am, undoubtedly, merely scratching the surface and preaching to the choir with these wonderful examples of how camp influences the lives of those individuals involved, but these life lessons and shared experiences promote the outcome of the everlasting bond that camp folk enjoy and internalize. Once a camper, always a camper.

I have enjoyed adapting to life outside of camp thanks to the lessons learned at camp. As such, I will forever be an ambassador for the industry. I eagerly await my return this year and the SLC conference was a much-needed spark to a wave of thoughts that I did not know I needed.

If Not for Paula

Jamie Yarow

I went to summer camp my whole life. Frankly, I loved everything about it. In the summer of 1976, I thought I would try resident camp for two weeks. The only person I knew at the camp was my 6th grade boyfriend. At the bus pick-up, he told me that he did not want to "go with me" anymore. As a result, for the next two hours, I sat alone on the bus, holding back the tears.

When I arrived at camp, I met my bunkmates. They had all been attending camp together for many summers, which definitely made me the outsider. Homesickness set in, and I hated everything. The kid who previously loved camp was now hating it.

Feeling all alone and ready to go home, I met a counselor named Paula. She took me under her wing. She invited me to join the other counselors to eat lunch. She took me over to the horses and let me help care for them. I began to love the experience. On the last day of camp, I cried. I was going to miss all the counselor friends I had met. I recently found Paula on Facebook and sent her this note:

> Hi Paula, You probably don't recall who I am, but I always remember the counselor at camp who was super nice to me, when all the other kids at camp were so mean. I wore a t-shirt that said "Support Your Local Hooker, Buy a Rug Today." My dad owned a carpet store. Does that ring a bell? Anyway, I wanted to thank you. Today, I'm a well-adjusted summer camp owner. I always tell my staff how important their actions are. I use my own story about how I hated camp, and it was the actions of one camp counselor who changed my experience. Look, it was over 30 years ago, and that one camp counselor is still making a difference!

The Canoe Adventure

Amanda Zoellner

This event happened early in my camp career, when I was still a seasonal staff member. This situation involved a canoe.

Every camper who wanted to go on a canoe trip got to go. To make sure that happened, in the third week of a four-week camp session, we took out two overnight trips, back to back, to a primitive campsite right on our lake. For these trips, the first group would leave from camp, paddle around the lake to the campsite, set up all the tents, make dinner, stay overnight, have breakfast, and return to camp before lunch.

My group would hop in the canoes with our food and personal gear, paddle to the campsite, make dinner, stay overnight, have breakfast, pack up all the tents and other group gear, and head back to camp. Sounds easy, right?

We had a series of checklists to prep for trips, and we followed them religiously. I had packed all the food for both groups. When I went to grab the breakfast pack for my group, however, it wasn't where I left it. I looked everywhere for it. One of the other staff members told me that the previous group had packed it, so I decided to trust that it would be there. After our day of paddling, we got to the campsite, moved into our tents, and made dinner. While the girls had their s'mores, I went through all the gear, looking for the breakfast pack. Of course, it wasn't there.

I was a bit panicked—campers with no breakfast, and I was the trip leader, which made the situation all my fault! I thought about hopping in a canoe and paddling back to camp to bring back some breakfast, or waking the girls early to get back to camp for breakfast there.

As was the tradition, however, we had brought dehydrated camping meals for dinner on our trip, but hadn't used the desserts, which served as my back-up plan. The chocolate pudding mix would become hot chocolate, and the dehydrated apple crisp was enough like oatmeal with fruit to call it breakfast. The next morning, the campers, expecting the traditional instant oatmeal, were surprised by the change in breakfast menu, but were more than happy to eat the alternative that we had prepared. Crisis averted.

We paddled back to camp, debriefed, and unpacked all the gear. The missing breakfast pack was eventually found in exactly the place it should have been. While I felt like a fool, but no campers went hungry or were endangered, I put the situation behind me. Two lessons learned—pack an extra meal, and always pack my own stuff!

A week later, when the first-session campers had left, but the second-session campers had not yet arrived, I came back to my bunk, after some time off, to find a little package and a note on my bed. It was from one of the campers who'd been on my trip. The gift parcel contained cookies from a local bakery, as well as a note.

She wrote that our camping trip had been her best trip ever. They'd had an adventure because of the missing breakfast food. For her, at 10 years old, it felt like a survival experience, and she thanked me for being such a great leader. She also told me that she thought I was so creative for making a special, tasty breakfast out of leftovers. She couldn't wait to go on her next canoe trip and have another adventure!

That incident taught me a few lessons that I've taken to heart in my time as a camp professional, including the following:

- It's easy to make too big a deal out of a relatively small thing, and to create a crisis unnecessarily.
- A small thing, that might seem insignificant, can also be a transformative experience.
- I was creative and could think outside the boundaries to solve problems.
- While it took a few more years after that summer to decide that camp would be my career, I still remember that spark that helped light my personal campfire. That camper is an adult now—I should find her and tell her that she made a difference for me!

Murph

Ian Moorhouse

I am sitting next to my new bride, my soul mate, on the most exciting day of my life. My best man is standing up in front of us, making an incredible speech about our 11-year friendship.

Flash back to the summer of 1997, Murph is 10 years old and wanders into the section of camp that I was in charge. The camp was a summer home for hundreds of children from low-income families. Murph and I had an instant connection. We both came from similar backgrounds and were complete goof balls. Murph followed me everywhere at camp. Because he never had enough clothes, on my days off, I would either try to buy him some or he would wear some of mine.

At the end of the session, I told the camp director that I wanted to donate my paycheck to cover the costs for Murph to come back. When I told Murph, he burst into tears. Murph came back the next session with a "best buddies" photo frame and a card thanking me. Every summer and every session after that summer, Murph came to camp, and we were inseparable.

When I moved to my present locale in 1999, Murph was in the big brother program. In more ways than one, I was very fortunate that I became his big brother. At my wedding, Murph talked about the impact that I had on him. Little does he know, however, that he had a greater impact on me, and that I am forever grateful for having a little brother whom I would never have had if it wasn't for him.

Scott's Staff

Todd Walker

I hung up my staff jacket many years ago, which was a jacket that I had idolized as a young Boy Scout just outside of Anchorage, AK. I wanted to wear a Camp Gorsuch staff jacket, not because I loved doing merit badges, because frankly I didn't. It was too much like school. I wanted to wear a Gorsuch staff jacket because of names like Yancy, Shamu, Baby T, Smokey, Zach, Art, and Betty.

There was one name, however, that made everyone want to wear a Gorsuch staff jacket—a name whose reputation caused applications to come in by the hundreds from across the country and the world. I wanted to wear a Gorsuch staff jacket because that meant I would be on Scott Powell's staff.

Scott took time to learn about every single one of the hundreds of campers who came through the gates every week all summer. You didn't even know he was doing it until the next year when you heard "Hey Todd, good to see ya!" You could hear him coming with his "yodel-ay-hee-hoo!"

He was the keeper of tradition and everything else at Gorsuch. He was the ranger who kept the lights and the water running. He was also the program director who kept the camp running. Furthermore, he was the man who kept the staff running.

I didn't even know he knew I was moving out of Alaska the summer after 8th grade. Nonetheless, he called me up in front of the whole camp one day at lunch to sing "Happy Trails" to me. I was too cool and too tough to cry at that age. But, I came close.

That winter, I turned 15, the age you could be on camp staff, but I was headed to Philmont. I'd wear that staff jacket next summer. Spring 2004, I had my phone interview with Scott. I made it on staff. All my friends did. We were going to be the next names that campers remembered forever. We were going to work for Scott Powell.

Staff week starts. Surprisingly, Scott doesn't work there anymore. The politics drove him out. Those of us who showed up to be on Scott's staff were suddenly working for someone else. We were now responsible for keeping alive all of the reasons to be on Scott's staff and go to Scott's camp.

It was easy the first year. The memories were fresh. Susie. Wadottenchew. The Erbie Walker. The Gorsuch Hymn. All of the traditions, all the stories were fresh in our minds.

The second year was a little tougher. Time meant you forgot the little things. Thankfully, Scott came back that year—just for a visit. It was the 50th anniversary of Camp Gorsuch.

When he came back, he brought a book of "Scott's Thoughts." All of his Scoutmaster minutes from over the years. The history of the camp. Why we do what we do. I knew that book, plus my "Gorsuch Pocket Radio" (the staff songbook), were valuable in keeping Scott's camp alive, but I didn't know how much.

That week he visited was the last time I ever saw Scott. He died two weeks later at the Boy Scout Jamboree in Virginia, along with several other members of our camp "family" in a freak accident that made national news. I didn't cry when he sent me off in 8th grade. I was too cool for that. This time, staffers I grew up wanting to be like cried. I did too.

For the years following, change was inevitable. We held onto Scott's traditions as tightly as we could. This was his camp. We wanted to be on his staff. We wanted to give those campers the same experience we had growing up. "Scott's Thoughts" were priceless.

When I started getting big-boy bills, I needed to get a big-boy job. Subsequently, I passed along the traditions I had guarded so tightly to the campers-turned-staffers who, for some reason, wanted to be like me. No matter who you were, Scott made you feel special. He made you feel like you mattered. I never got to be on Scott's staff. Hopefully, however, I did him proud.

Foster Sister Reunion

Donna Johns-Thomas

In the summer of 2001, I was directing an all-girls overnight camp in Michigan. I participated in a pilot program that enabled girls from the foster care system and battered women's shelters to have a camp experience. It was pretty amazing, as well as quite an undertaking. The girls had backstories that ran the gamut. For me, however, a pair of sisters really stood out.

About mid-season, I got a call from one of the social workers I dealt with, asking if I had room for two girls, ages 6 and 10. She further asked if the girls could be in the same group together, given that they were sisters. I explained that because our camp groups campers aged six to eight together, and aged 9 to 11 together, it wouldn't be possible for them to be in the same group. Initially, I didn't think this situation would be an issue, because we have many siblings who come to camp the same week who aren't in the same group. I had no idea what the social worker was about to say next:

"Please can you make an exception? They're sisters, but we weren't able to place them in the same foster home. They adore one another … and they haven't seen each other in over two years. I've been trying to arrange time for them to be together, but due to the foster families' distance from one another and time constraints, we just haven't been able to make it happen. Having them come to camp together for a whole week would be more than they could dream of. Furthermore, the older sister is more than willing to be with the younger group. Please?"

I said "yes" immediately. I met with the staff team that I planned to place them with to explain why a 10 year old would be with next week's group. I didn't expect the near-mutiny in store for me:

"Are you actually telling us that you expect us to facilitate this grand reunion … and then reinjure their little hearts by tearing them apart and sending them to different homes again at the end of the week? We refuse. We won't do it. That's just cruel to them and cruel to us."

Once I picked my jaw off the floor, I explained, "Yes, you will do it, because you're professionals, and this is your job. But, beyond that, just consider this … at least you're giving them this week together. It's not forever. It doesn't fix their lives. But, it is one week more than they had before. At least, they'll have a week. What a gift you're giving them." Eventually, the counselors tearfully and with some trepidation, relented.

The girls arrived the next week, and I have to say that they were two of the sweetest girls I've ever had as campers. They had a WONDERFUL time. I checked in on them a lot that week (and checked in on their counselors too). They thoroughly enjoyed camp and their time with one another. They also made scores of new friends.

The day before they left, they came up to me at the camp office hand in hand, and (no lie) thanked me for letting them be together. "We had so much fun! Thank you for letting us be in the same group!"

Much to the amazement of the staff and myself, when it came time to leave the next day … it wasn't the dramatic parting everyone feared. A couple little tears, a really big hug, and an "I miss you and I love you."

Right after they left, the lead counselor … the one who was going to quit before having them in her group … said to me, through very misty eyes, "Those two are why we do what we do." I couldn't agree more.

THE MILLENNIAL BLOGOSPHERE

monkeybusinessimages/iStock/Thinkstock

As I was working on the final edits to this book, I happened upon a blog posting from a woman names Sydney Collins entitled, "A Thank-You Letter To My Camp" or "Camp Rocks" for short. This is what she wrote:

Dear Camp,

For some, we've spent the past eight years basking in the sun and life that is on Moose Pond. No matter when you come into this wondrous camp, you're welcomed with open arms and a "hello." The love I've felt from every single camper and counselor is an unparalleled feeling and has affected me in many ways, all for the better.

We all come from different walks of life, with different stories and diverse and beautiful personalities that somehow mold together to create the enduring bond that we now all officially share. Saying "thank you" simply feels like an understatement. I am forever indebted to every person there.

I will always treasure the memories we've made dancing in the Wiggie, hiking up Pleasant Mountain, canoeing, singing at the Cobb and Evening Circle, and just being happy to be in each other's company.

Not only has each and every camper emotionally touched me in some way, but my counselors have been a big part of my growing up. You've taught me how to be a strong, smart, independent, and truly happy person. Through your life lessons and stories, you've helped me become comfortable in my own skin and embrace who I am.

I sincerely thank the world every day for bringing me there to the shores and letting me be a part of this beautiful tradition of camp.

The scenic landscape the camp rests on could alone make you shake with emotion. I remember waking up especially early sometimes and seeing the water laying so flat that the mountain that rested above it had a perfectly mirrored reflection in the water. Sometimes, the clouds hung so low that they seemed to become part of Pleasant Mountain. The sunsets truly define what heaven's door is supposed to look like— ranging in color from a hot pink to bright orange. At night, the stars were so bright and present that they completely contrasted with the pitch black sky behind it.

Trying to experience everything this wondrous place had to offer is a feat in itself. But like everyone else, I really did try to taste it all. At nights, by lamplight, my cabinmates and I would sit and try to solve problems too vexing for 13-year-old minds (though at the time, it felt like we were solving world hunger). Our counselors would join in and give us lessons from their wiser minds. Everyone seems to be trying to find their place of peace in this crazy world, and I am so happy and grateful that I was able to find mine. So to the mountain, the shores, the Wiggie, the Cobb, and everyone who shares in my love for camp, I say thank you.

Sincerely,

Sydney Collins

After reading her letter, I thought to myself, that's it! That's exactly what I've been looking for in compiling this book. So I reached out to Sydney and asked her permission to reprint her wonderful letter in this book.

It was at this point I discovered the platform where she posted her original piece. It is an online forum called The Odyssey Online and is self-described as follows:

Hi. We're Odyssey
We are a content platform that discovers and shares a chorus
of millennial voices on topics that matter most to you.
Odyssey enables content to find its most relevant audience organically.
www.theodysseyonline.com

I surfed a bit and to my pleasant surprise found a multitude of posts about summer camp from a community I had often regarded as too young and/or too into themselves to truly value the magic of the summer camp experience. I have been gratefully proven wrong, as the next few pages will reveal.

*A special thanks to the Odyssey admin team who
granted permission to reprint this content.

Summer Camp Changed My Life

Taylor Zavodnick

Like many other children during the summer, I went to summer camp. I couldn't wait for camp to start. To me, summer meant camp. Every summer, the first day of camp was as exciting as Christmas morning for me. I was a pretty average kid, with very average skills. There was nothing special about me. But, this camp truly changed my life.

The camp that I went to is called Adventureland Day Camp, and it is located in Bensalem, PA. It is a beautiful piece of land, with a lake and the Neshaminy Creek, as well as a rock wall, a zip line, pools, and so much more. I started there when I was about four years old.

Some of my best memories happened at this camp. I learned skills in sports and improved the skills I already had. I learned how to do new activities, such as archery. I was taught how to swim, and found a new love for the water. I soon became a great swimmer, due to my daily swim lessons. I loved the water so much that when I was old enough, I became a certified lifeguard.

My love for nature and the outdoors grew. I remember going on nature walks through the woods and noticing things that I never knew before. I learned names of plants and how to identify them (leaves of three, let it be!). I got dirty and grimy, and I loved every second of it. I learned how to take fish and turtles off of my line, once I caught one. I learned the importance of being aware of safety, because some things at camp can be dangerous.

I became better at making friends, because I did not live in the immediate area of camp. Therefore, I did not go to school with the kids who went to the camp. This situation forced me to go out of my comfort zone and make friends. These individuals became lifelong friends.

I learned that you might not enjoy every activity, but some people won't like the things that you enjoy. Everyone has his or her own likes and dislikes, and that's OK. This factor forces you to take a step back and look at things a different way. I started to participate more in the things that I "didn't like," which made me realize that if you give things a chance, you may be surprised.

I always felt accepted at my camp. I was always a "bigger" child and struggled with my weight and confidence my entire life. At camp, however, that didn't matter. There were kids of every background, class, race, ability, size, shape, etc. This camp became my second home.

When I got older, I decided I wanted to work at camp. What an experience this responsibility has been. Somehow, I have learned even more from this place as an employee, than I did as a camper. Now, I can work with other people, even if I don't particularly like them. I can think outside the box. Sometimes, it is hard to get kids to do something. Finding a fun and creative way to get them to do what you ask of them is a great skill to know.

On top of everything I learned at camp, I think that it just made me an all-around better person. I do not think that I would be as accepting, patient, willing to try new things, creative, and so much more if I didn't spend my summers at camp.

Thank you to my summer camp for changing my life for the better.

Why I Spend My Summer as a Camp Counselor

Sydney Sutton

Being a camp counselor is the best job ever. Whenever I'm asked what my first job was, my answer is that I was a camp counselor. When asked what I do each summer, my answer is always the same: I am a camp counselor. Some people give me a look of happiness, while others give me a look of fear. Many people have had the opportunity to be camp counselors, while others have not. I believe being a camp counselor is the best job ever. I wouldn't trade it for the world.

Being a camp counselor is not as easy as it seems. You have to wake up before your campers and go to staff meetings. You will get very little sleep. You will be tired 24/7. You have to have patience with each and every camper. You have to eat the same food each week for a month. You sometimes grow tired of being around children. You sing the same songs over and over again. Coffee becomes your best friend at staff meetings. You are always late. Always. You take cabin kickback (nap time) seriously. Nonetheless, although it can be difficult, being a camp counselor is very rewarding in the long run.

Through spending my summer as a camp counselor, I have met some awesome campers who have changed my life forever. One thing that brings a smile to my face is seeing my campers so happy to learn about the Gospel. It makes me very happy that the girls enjoy the camp and the activities that we do. The discussions I have had with my campers have helped me build a personal relationship with them, while planting a seed in their life. I love watching the girls look at us counselors in awe, as we teach them during round table discussion or when we are practicing the memory verse with them.

Through working as a camp counselor for multiple weeks, I have the ability to meet many different counselors and serve with them. It is extremely enjoyable to work with other individuals who are as passionate about the camp and its ministry as you are. Growing relationships with the fellow counselors, even after camp is over, provides me with forever friends. The weekends when the campers aren't there are some of the most memorable moments, whether it be staying up late playing games or midnight Sonic runs to get a Nerds Slushie. I will always cherish the relationships that I have made over the years with my fellow counselors.

Spirit day is by far my favorite day of the week. After spending several weeks at camp, you are put on different teams. Nothing beats watching the girls work together to beat the other team in the different games. Dressing up in your team's color is always very competitive. Each counselor always tries to outdo the other.

Water games day is also a very fun and memorable time. Having a group of little girls come up to you and ask you specifically to go down the huge slip 'n' slide makes me feel extremely special. The girls enjoy this day almost as much as spirit day. For the girls who do not go down the slip 'n' slide, it is a great opportunity to talk to them about what they have been learning in Chapel.

The most important reason I spend each and every summer as a camp counselor is because of the mission of the camp. Providing several hundred children with the opportunity to hear the Gospel and accept Jesus Christ as their Savior is a life-changing event. Being a part of changing a child's life is amazing. Reuniting with a camper after not seeing them for a year warms your heart. Nothing makes me smile more than when a camper tells me that I am their role model and that they love me.

There really is no job like being a summer camp counselor.

An Open Letter to the Summer Camp That Helped Me Grow

Mary Rom

One of the best places in existence—we all have that one thing in our life that we can never let go of. Whether it is people, places, or things, we'd do anything to make sure it never leaves us. In this instance, my thing is my sleep-away camp, which I attended for five years.

Every summer that I attended, I was always happy to be there. Regardless of everything that was going on in my life, my summers were always filled with happiness and joy. When I started, I was 14 years old. Last year, was my final summer attending (although I hope to sneak in for some more), and I could not be more grateful.

The more summers I went there, the more I felt myself growing. The person I was when I first started and the person I am now are two somewhat different people. To change isn't necessarily a bad thing. As long as you don't lose yourself when you're changing, that's all that matters.

During my time at camp, I've had people look up to me, and I've had people to whom I looked up. In fact, I continue to admire many of them. Being in an atmosphere where the world isn't a dark and scary place should be something everyone at least experiences once in a lifetime.

My time at camp may be over, but I will never forget the people and the memories I've made. Although I'm not a camper anymore, it's gonna take a lot more than my age to get rid of me. Having this experience has taught me a lot. It has helped me make friendships with people all over the world.

It has been my own Neverland. Being in camp has made me never want to grow up. Here's to you, Southampton Freshair Home. Thank you for everything.

Why I Love Being a Camp Counselor

Amanda Bohlmann

Although, at times, it is stressful, there is no other summer job I would rather have than being a camp counselor. When deciding on choosing to work at a camp, there were a lot of things that ran through my mind. Did I really want to spend my summer waking up at 7:30 a.m.? Did I want to spend eight hours a day, five days a week, out in the scorching hot sun, chasing kids around? Did I want to give up doing activities during the week, because I knew I would be too tired after work every day to go out? A million questions ran through my mind, when I thought about being a camp counselor for the summer.

While I still did not have the answers to those questions, I decided to just go for it. I knew that I would still get to have a summer for two months before camp started. Because I never went to a traditional camp as a kid, I wanted to have the experience.

Now that I'm in my fourth week of camp as a counselor, I have found the answers to my million questions that I had asked myself. Yes, I absolutely want to spend eight hours a day, five days a week, out in the scorching hot sun chasing kids around. Yes, I am okay with giving up weekday activities; I could always do them on the weekend. Yes, I want to spend my summer waking up at 7:30 a.m. (in reality, I'm still trying to work on that one). All of the things I was worried about have left my mind.

I love every second of being a camp counselor. I love being outside all day running around. It sure beats staying at home and lying on the couch, watching TV all day. There is nothing more rewarding than watching the kids in my group excel. Each child will have that one activity that they seem to struggle with, and it is the greatest feeling in the world getting to see them get better and better at it each day.

Counselors are role models to the campers. I didn't realize how true that was until I became a counselor and got to experience it. My campers show up to camp every day with big smiles, excited to see their counselors. They run toward us as soon as they get out of their cars. As we walk from activity to activity, they run to hold my hand, and we chat about how their night was as we walk. When it is time for dismissal, they all make sure to give hugs to all of their counselors before they leave. These kids really look up to their counselors.

It is a big responsibility to look after kids. Although it is a job, there really is not a big difference between campers and counselors. Counselors are just campers at heart. We get more into the themed days than the campers do. I have a great time at work and have fun while doing so.

At the end of the day, when I come home exhausted, smelling of suntan lotion and chlorine, I realize that there is no other summer job that I would rather have. I love being a camp counselor and wouldn't trade it for the world.

Why I'm Thankful for My Summer Camp Experiences— Hello Mother, Hello Father

Gabi Bon Durant

Having grown up as an only child of a single parent, I was very sheltered. For the majority of my life, my closest friend was my mom. Fortunately for me, while I was growing up, I was blessed with the opportunity to go to summer camp (a luxury many other low-income families, unfortunately, can't afford). From the age of five, I went to day camp, where my days consisted of hours of arts and crafts, fun field trips, and water play. I made new friends whom I didn't see at school, I bonded with my counselors and got to make hotdogs shaped like octopi and slime made out of cornstarch, borax, and food dye. To say my days at day camp were anything but bliss would be the understatement of the century, until they ended around the age of nine.

When I turned nine and was deemed a "big kid," I got the opportunity to go to sleep-away camp. I believe that it was at this time that my anxiety toward the unknown was triggered. What's most interesting about the social experiment that is sleep-away camp is that different kids often have different reactions. Some kids can't wait to go; a break from their home life is welcomed. Other kids are a little ambivalent, but otherwise don't mind the change. Still other children, like me, were visibly uneasy about the thought of spending four nights per session away from their home and parents.

As embarrassing as it is to admit today, I had major anxiety attacks and irrational fears associated with going to camp. Nothing particularly traumatizing happened to me, except a profound sense of homesickness that thankfully I worked through. With the help of my tremendously patient and loving mom and my wonderfully attentive counselors, I was able to tackle my fears head-on, while learning to love camp. I attribute a lot of who I am today to the experiences that I had while away in the Hollywood Hills at summer camp.

I'm thankful for the experience of camp, because it allowed me to come home to a newly decorated and de-cluttered room. I am thankful for camp, because it helped me to become more independent. I am thankful for camp, because it prepared me to transition to college. I am thankful to camp, because I can travel unaccompanied by my mom and feel self-assured. I am thankful for my camp experience, because it has taught me to be more selfless. I am thankful for camp for giving me the opportunity to pay it forward by being a camp counselor as my first job, when I was 19 years old. While the initial experience was uncomfortable, and I was a crying hot mess, clinging to care-packages from home, it allowed me to grow as a person and is an experience that I'll never forget!

Note: There's LOTS more on theodysseyonline.com website.

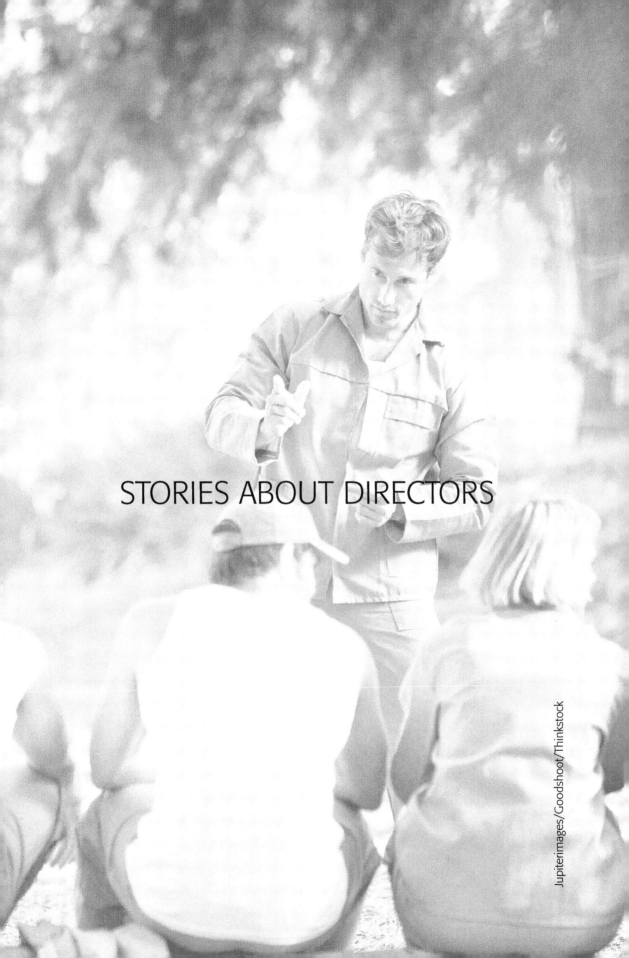

STORIES ABOUT DIRECTORS

Starlord

Sarah Resch

Last summer, we hired a 17 year old to work an hourly position in the kitchen. This young man interviewed well and had a great personality, though he was very open about hating school. "Hate it" is not too strong of a description. He really hates it. This child was diagnosed with Asperger's Syndrome in 8th grade after years of IEPs and testing and being diagnosed by teachers with oppositional defiance disorder. He tried a number of ADHD medications, none of which seemed to make a difference in his school performance. Eventually, his parents took him off all medication in the 7th grade. His camp supervisor was told about his Asperger's Syndrome and that he was an introvert, who displayed some social awkwardness, but otherwise was very high functioning.

Two days into staff training, this employee had a camp name, "Starlord. Furthermore, he was fully immersed with camp staff, sharing stories during staff training, giving his opinion, and asking questions alongside all of his college-aged peers. This young man was all smiles and made friends quickly.

His kitchen supervisor throughout the summer named Starlord as the best early morning employee, because he was never late even when he was assigned the dreaded 6:30 a.m. shift. Starlord volunteered for evening program duties and loved caring for the petting farm animals over the weekend for the petting farm specialist. Camp staff and campers alike embraced him.

One night, Starlord expressed that he had never had close friends like this and he couldn't wait to be in college like his camp staff friends. It was a huge AHA moment for him when a friend expressed "Dude, you don't have to be in college to have friends like this. You just have to choose the kind of friends that you can be like this with." LIGHT BULB! Suddenly, this young man had a place where he fit and he KNEW that he could find others who fit with him back at school.

The end of the summer arrived, and Starlord was in tears, saying goodbye just like all of his fellow camp staff members and campers. After the last bus was waved to, the last cabin was cleaned and locked up, and the last staff member's beat-up car had left the parking lot, Starlord hopped on the golf cart with his mom, the executive director of camp and said. "Mom, I want to go major in recreation management and be a camp director so that all kids can have a place to be."

You see, my son Alex has always been on the outside of a group. Becoming Starlord helped him see that he has choices in the person that he is. Hearing about struggles from his camp staff friends was a bigger lesson than another mom or dad talk ever could be. Camp changed my son. Camp improved my son. Camp helped my son see the importance of giving back to others. Amazing.

Lessons From a Beer Can

Jenny McMillian

The camp director was fired, and I was asked to take his place. Another key staff member quit, and it seemed things were going from bad to worse.

I felt like a firefighter going from one situation to the next, trying to work out issues as they flared up. As I walked in to my new office, I saw a very large Fosters beer can on my desk. There was a post-it note on top that covered the fact that it was already opened. I giggled as I thought how nice it would be to drink a very large beer at the moment. On the other hand, with a strict rule of no alcohol in camp, it was more alarming than promising.

I picked up the empty can and read the note. "Found on recycle bin." I looked up to see a few leaders staring at me through my open door.

It hit me what it must look like as I stood there with a beer can in my hand tilted forward to read the note. I just smiled as I set the can down. I realized that I needed to address this matter in the leader meeting that was starting in 15 minutes. Once again, I had another issue to extinguish.

I gathered up what I needed for the meeting, beer can included, and headed out. The leaders were all there as I rounded the corner and saw their surprised looks at the large beer can I was holding. I set it down first and then the rest of the material I had. I introduced myself. I joked at my surprise and disappointment in finding an empty beer can on my desk. They seemed relieved that I wasn't hitting the bottle at 9 a.m. in this youth camp. They were caught off guard, however, when I announced that one of THEIR co-leaders or parents were drinking in the camp. I was met with instant denial by the entire group. One leader reacted with, "No way! That was a youth!" I reminded them that it was found on the recycle bin. No underage kid is going to recycle a beer can.

If a child did manage to smuggle in beer, the can would have been hidden in the woods somewhere. Only an adult without proper training would not realize that alcohol use is forbidden at camp. Once the realization set it, you could see their minds racing. Each of them feared it could be one of their people.

I reassured them that we were not "head hunting," and I would rely on their leadership to handle this. I told them that it was not as important to find out who did it, as it was to ensure that it didn't happen again. I advised them to go back to their campsites and not accuse anyone, but to engage in an impromptu youth protection training session, emphasizing the importance of having no alcohol or tobacco in camp. Frankly, I was sure that whoever did drink the beer had no knowledge that doing so violated our policies, because they walked right up in a very public area and recycled the can.

Other directors may have pointed fingers and stirred up issues that would light lots of fires, but that day, using humor and patience, I made it a learning opportunity. I also gained the respect of several leaders, who became my firefighting brethren.

Camp Magic

Erin Johnson

There is always talk of the camp magic and how it impacts campers and staff alike. There are a number of conversations that take place between campers and staff about which staff they most admire, who secretly and for some publicly want to be like. I was almost seven years old when I started at camp. I was beyond excited. I loved the independence and the choices that I was allowed and encouraged to make.

I am not sure about anyone else's counselors, but mine had magic abilities, they could make up a song out of two words, comforting me in a way that only my parents had done before. I felt very safe in this new environment. In this place, I was encouraged to try new things; especially those things that made my tummy feel a little funny inside.

When you are seven, all counselors are heroes and bigger than life. In reality, some of them had barely seen the beginning of their 18th year.

That very first summer, my hero was named Flipper. She was so nice. She could sing camp songs and could create and play endless games. She also held our hands when we walked back to our cabins in the dark. I remember coming home that year and telling my parents that I wanted to work at camp and be just like her.

As the years went by, we both got older and grew up more and more. She would go on to be part of the administrative team for the camp and eventually the camp director. I continued on as a camper and participating in the leadership program. I loved the idea of being the camp director one day—wow, what a job that would be! What could be better than to have a walkie-talkie and have campers get so excited to see you. At that point, life would be perfect.

Over time, my path in life ebbed and flowed, while camp remained a strong constant. I continued up the camp staff ladder, until one day the opportunity of a lifetime, one that I didn't realize I wanted and maybe even needed, came to be. I was appointed as the camp director of the camp that I attended as a child. One of the best things said to me at the time came from my first counselor, who stated that she was so proud of the person I had become.

Pass Me By

Sara & Gwynn Powell

Growing up in a family that owned and operated a summer camp, you hear lots of stories. I've been collecting stories since I was small. I've also burned letters with a camper whose dad sent sarcastic notes saying he didn't' miss her, and dried her tears as they went up in smoke. I've introduced people to their future wives, intentionally believing that they would be a good fit. I've sobbed over the death of campers, whose lives were brief and brilliant. All of the minutia that happen on a day-to-day basis solidified my choice to be involved in camping, and grounded me every season. Camp is my literal home, where I grew up, but also my heart home.

In the summer of 2011, I asked JRC alumni to speak to our new staff. I reached out to so many people, but Alyssa K's response was the one that broke my heart and healed it, all in one moment.

Alyssa grew up in Bakersfield, and she was at camp on a trade. Her dad had a carpet cleaning business, and we needed what he had, and Alyssa needed what we provided. Alyssa came to camp year after year, during which time, I was her counselor. I tucked her in to bed every night and "snorged" in her ear (i.e., the sound pigs make). She'd giggle uncontrollably every time. I gave her back rubs, when she first got into bed, made sure that she was happy, and helped her control her hair—all of the things I was told helps kids be more comfortable at camp.

I was away at college when she was on staff, but visited her often. On occasion, we talked for only a few moments, but the reconnections were beautiful. When the 75th reunion came around, Alyssa and I were at the campfire, and she said something like, "I want to sing with my idol, Erica J, tonight." I remember blushing. Alyssa has an amazing voice, and to sing next to her was both a treat and honor.

The following is a partial recollection of what Alyssa said:

> "[The counselors] instilled a confidence in me that I didn't otherwise have. They saw things in me that I didn't know were there ... they allowed me to identify myself and my abilities in a much broader way than I would have ever done, on my own. I wasn't a kid who was necessarily 'bullied,' but something close to it. I used to dream during the school year about those summers, where I would have adults who didn't bully me, like my teachers did, when I would meet other kids ... who were open to me and my ideas. Where I had the opportunity to be amongst a group of people who loved me from the second I showed up, just for being me, and who told me that I could be more than I conceived for myself."

If I never do anything else in life, her comments alone make camp worth it. This inarguably confirms what I do, what I choose every year. The power of this is staggering, and I'm honored to be even a little part of it.

At the end of each camp session, we put on a performance for the camper parents. One group, in particular, had been challenging, because we were in the beginning of understanding how to mainstream campers. The group had eight campers, including one child with cerebral palsy. The skit looked something like the following:

The entire cabin group assisted the camper with a disability to a chair in the middle of the stage and then arranged themselves around and behind her. One of the counselors explained that their cabin had had a very special time and had learned so many life lessons that went well beyond horseback, archery, and crafts. The counselor explained that the group experienced the learning process of understanding what the camper with special needs could do on her own and learning what she needed assistance with and how to tell the difference.

The entire group then smiled and began to sing, "Pass Me By." While this happened in 1972, camper parents, to this day, still talk about how they don't remember the entire song or what their own child's camper groups did on stage, but these words ring loud and clear:

> I've got me 10 fine toes to wiggle in the sand
> Lots of idle fingers jump to my command …
> And if you don't happen to like it,
> Deal me out, thank you kindly, pass me by.

The girl in the chair acted out as many of the lyrics as well as she could, and her cabin mates joined her. There was not a dry eye left in the building by the time they finished. Everyone learned a valuable lesson. In fact, the value of capitalizing on the teachable moments that were beyond the scheduled camp program made all the difference for those campers and the entire camp.

The Einstein Award

Sherri Pacitto

I was sent to camp at a very young age. I went to preschool camp, day camp, and then to sleep- away camp for a month, when I was just turning nine years old. It was for a whole month. I believed my mother hated me and that's why she sent me away to camp. Actually I don't think that was really true, but I believed it with all my heart at the time.

At camp, I learned to ride a horse from a cowboy named Lucky. He taught me to trick ride, which is when I got a tiny glimpse of a wondrous kid who loved to learn and wanted to try everything. I also became a "star" at this camp, playing Laurie in the musical Oklahoma. I practiced and practiced, and then practiced some more for the role. I felt cared about, as well as accepted and lifted, for the first time in my life. I learned all kinds of amazing things at camp. I sang songs at breakfast, lunch, and dinner. I placed my gum on the coolest gum tree ever, as I entered the waterfront area. I water-skied every day. I sailed. I learned how to roll a canoe. I also learned a lifelong passion of crafting. I remember making my first pair of copper-fused glass earrings. I still have them, still wear them, and am still proud that I made them myself.

At that camp, I felt like I belonged, and I felt loved. I remember at the last campfire before the parents came to pick up their kids at the end of the month, the director, Sulie, sang "No Man is an Island." Furthermore, we all got to put our handprints in the concrete sidewalk around camp. I cried my heart out that I would have to go home, but I carried those sweet amazing memories and all the new skills I had learned with me.

I went to that camp for three years. That experience has carried me through life emotionally. I went back and worked at that camp through college and went on to work at several other camps throughout the past 30 years. If I hadn't gone to that camp, I'm not certain I would be in the position I am in today. The skills I learned at the Harand Camp of the Theatre Arts have helped me through some of the most difficult times of my life.

I want to give all of those sweet amazing memories to other children going forward in my life. When I first arrived at camp, I felt broken, but camp made me whole again. I learned both communication skills and leadership skills. I tested myself physically and found that I could dance and sing, design and sew costumes, memorize huge scripts, as well as ride a horse and take care of it. Honestly, the list is really immense. Today, I have guts and determination. I also have integrity, persistence, and perseverance. I am tenacious and have achieved every goal I have ever set for myself. Without camp, I would not be who I am today!

Once, I met an extraordinary young boy who was very precious. I enjoyed getting to know him. He was painfully shy and would keep to himself most of the time. He was also much smaller than most of the other children and would get knocked down quite a bit when we were playing games. He was also resilient and observant. I watched him for a day or two and discovered he was extraordinarily smart.

I particularly watched him when we did an experiment with dry ice. He knew all the chemical compounds and actually taught the other kids why dry ice was like fog in the bubbles we had made. The next day, we had a science teacher come to our camp to do some special experiments.

Every time the teacher would ask a question, this five-year-old boy would shoot his hand in the air. Soon, it was a game for everyone, because this child knew the answer to every single question, and explained it to the class. In the process, everyone found out how amazing this little boy's mind was. Arguably, he was a genius. To everyone's amazement, this child knew every element, their corresponding number, and all of their properties on the chemistry chart.

No one wanted to answer any more questions, because they looked forward to his answers and waited for him to raise his quiet, sweet hand so that they could listen to what he had to say. At the end of the week, all the kids gave him a standing ovation when we presented him with the Einstein award. He beamed with pride, acceptance, and caring. I will cherish that moment forever, because that child has found his personal power and self-esteem. Camp rocks!

Daring Boys to Become Men

Dale Decker

Camp changed my life. Before camp, I was an overweight kid from the trailer parks of a poor, disadvantaged city, Oxnard, CA, with huge self-confidence issues. I was verbally and physically abused at home, and bullied at school. My home was the typical broken home—a workaholic/alcoholic fsather and a mother who was more into her own vice(s) than her kids. During my time at Pyles Camp, It was the first instance that a male role model told me something as simple as "good job!" My counselor, Wizard, whom I felt truly cared about me, took the time to listen to my problems. Pyles Camp became the family for which I always longed.

If it wasn't for camp, I know that eventually I would be a suicide statistic—I was already having the thoughts concerning whether the world would be a better place without me a part of it. I was already formulating a plan on how I would end it all.

If it wasn't for my experiences at Pyles Boys Camp, I would not be the individual I am today. Furthermore, I would not have lived the experiences I have been blessed to have, including lettering in football, participating in competitive cheerleading in high school, and receiving a college scholarship for cheerleading. From there, I had the opportunity to pursue my dreams of working in Hollywood as an associate producer for reality television shows.

I have graduated with a 3.5 GPA in organizational leadership from Cal Lutheran University. While camp didn't teach me everything, it did teach me to handle anything. Because of camp, I got to see the birth of my first child with my wonderful wife. I tribute all my life success to camp. Not only did it give me the confidence to live my life to the fullest, it also provided me with a strong work ethic to accomplish my goals, with the requisite drive to never give up.

Camp is extremely important in today's society. To quote Frederick Douglass, "It is easier to build strong children than to repair broken men." At Pyles Camp, we feel that we do this by daring boys to become men.

SUMMER CAMP STORIES FROM
THE FAR SIDE OF THE WORLD

While the embers from the log fire
Flicker, fly, and twirl
Then drift off toward the cosmos
From the Far Side of the World.

— Lyrics from the Far Side of
the World by Jimmy Buffett

In April of 2011, I had the opportunity to attend my first ACA Spring leadership Conference in Palm Springs, CA. The conference was held at what was then the Hotel Zoso (today it is the Hard Rock Hotel). One of the keynote speakers was an individual named Phil Lilienthal. He was a life-long camp professional from Camp Winnebago in Fayette, Maine. He was speaking on his most recent endeavor, Camp Sizanani in South Africa.

As I listened to his talk, I kept thinking two things: how cool it was that he had brought the American summer camp experience to the children of South Africa; and how I could totally see myself in that sort of role at some future point in my career.

Sometime after he spoke, we both found ourselves out at the hotel pool, presumably during the conference lunch break that day. We actually met in the water, both with a drink in our hand. I told him how much I appreciated the things he had said and how powerfully he communicated his obvious passion. We then spoke for the next three hours.

If either of us had planned to attend other conference sessions that afternoon, those plans quickly dissolved in the wake of our conversation. When we finally did wrap it up, he invited me to attend a session of Camp Sizanani as an international visiting staffer. I thought about that offer for the next several months.

Subsequently, we spoke again in October, when I called him and asked if the offer was still good. He replied, "Absolutely." At that point, I began preparations to head to the South African summer camp in December.

Those individuals who know me will quickly tell you of my fondness for Jimmy Buffett music and my parrothead adventures. One of his songs became my theme song for this journey: "Far Side of the World." I played it all the time (and still do), as I prepared for my trip. The two sets of lines that most speak to my soul are:

> I'm halfway round the planet,
> In a most unlikely place.
> —and—
> On the threshold of adventure,
> God I do love this job so.

I could write a completely separate book about my adventure to Camp Sizanani and working with the HIV/AIDS effected kids in Soweto (and maybe one day I will), but the following "short-list" outlines my adventure:

Camp Sizanani

Michael Jacobus

- I almost backed-out. Last minute nerves and that inner voice saying, 'What the hell are you doing?" got pretty loud up until departure time.
- It was the longest plane flight of my life getting there and even longer getting home—Atlanta to Johannesburg (17 hours)—return flight (21 hours).
- It took two-days of recovery time from jetlag (lots of soccer on every TV channel in South Africa at 2 a.m.).
- I pre-connected with several individuals from the local geocaching community. Not only did I make several new friends, I also received a local's tour of the area.
- I arrived at the predetermined meeting place and signed-in on the list of camp staff. I experienced a degree of culture shock, when reading the names of my fellow staffers:

Kabelo	Nkosana	Jabu	Bafana
Enos	Bongani	Nthabi	Michael (*there I am!*)
Sfiso	Xolani	Bruce	Lesedi
Siphiwe	Phumlani	Babalwa	Koketso

- Staff training was very similar to others I've attended, with a slight twist on topics like nutrition & life skills.
- My second culture shock occurred on the second morning of my training, when I had a hard time recognizing several of the female staff. Suffice it to say that was my first introduction to hair-weaves, extensions, and full-on wigs being worn by camp staff. For example, the young woman who had long blonde hair yesterday was bald today and would be a shorthaired brunette tomorrow. It took me a while to get up to speed.
- We were told that on the third or fourth day, everyone would likely be crying. I thought to myself, "that's kind of a weird statement. Why will everyone be crying?" Subsequently, I found out. On average, the kids who attend Camp Sizanani reach such a comfort lever by the third or fourth day that they begin to open up about their life experiences. It is indeed a powerful, wonderful, awful, gut-wrenching, and heartbreaking experience. We all cried. (You could have put the weeping on the camp schedule.)
- The campers and staff sing everywhere they go. Never in my life have I met people with more reason to feel beaten-down and worthless, who, instead, display a greater passion for life and joy than any others I know. It was truly a life-changing experience.
- Since returning, I have sponsored two members of my staff to take the same journey and participate as international visitor staffers. I have also had occasion to welcome six South African camp staffers to come visit or work for me here in California.

Needless to say, Phil and I have become good friends, and I am always excited to spend time with him and his staff at camp conferences. I asked him if he would provide a story for this book, as well. The following is Phil's story:

Why I Do What I Do

Philip Lilienthal

The dream had existed since 1967, when Lynn and I were Peace Corps volunteers in Ethiopia and I started a residential summer camp for boys. I wasn't sure whether the excitement of having started this camp or the impact it seemed to make on the young people who attended, was the measure of my personal achievement, but I loved the feeling.

After two summers of running this camp, we returned home, like most PCVs, with the fond memory of our experience and a vague readiness for what would come next. The feeling never went away. In my mind, I had developed a format for additional camps in Africa and had every intention of returning.

It took a good friend to tell me, nearly 30 years later, that if I wanted to do this, I should, and if I didn't want to, that would be fine, but please stop talking about it. It moved me to action. I had operated Camp Winnebago since 1974 and had grown it to exactly where I wanted, both in facilities and camp size. I loved every aspect of it.

It was time to move on, however. We had a family meeting to discuss who, if any, of our three children would be interested in pursuing camp as a career. At that point, I had a successor, a three-year transition plan, and a commitment to my next career, a camp in Africa.

The establishment of the camp was more like finding a partner who would be on the ground and run the day-to-day camp operations, as we would not be moving there. We also needed a site. I went to South Africa, Botswana, and Kenya in May 2003, looking for a partner organization. Africa had changed dramatically since 1967, and I found a lot of people who got the camp concept and a lot of sites that would be an enormous step up from where we started in 1966.

Michelle was my South African counterpart. She had budgets and a design for camp that were stunningly similar to my own. She had been turned down by two large international NGOs that asked for feasibility studies and needs assessment. I think she was shocked when I came in, ready for action.

Once we formalized our partnership in June, she asked when I wanted to get started. I suggested December, over the South African long school break. She was incredulous, "THIS December?" I replied, why not?

One of the things I wanted camp to have was an HIV/AIDS focus. South Africa had (and has) more people with HIV than any country in the world. I was consumed with trying to reduce the numbers, at least for our group.

Since HIV is brought on by so many other social factors, we had to educate not just on how it is transmitted, but the many aspects of it, such as the need for money, the feeling you owe something to your uncle who is providing food, the limited vision of opportunities that are available, the gender biases that exist, and the male role of dominance. Therefore, our camp curriculum would have to be weighted to have a strong life-skills focus.

Too many details to wade through, but we had our first staff training in December 2003. The campers were scheduled to arrive in early January. The remarkable Michael Brandwein said, "Yes" when I asked him if he would conduct our staff training. What a difference the five days with Michael made on the staff culture. We are still products of this amazing trainer, even 12 years later.

The most amazing thing was when the first camp was over. Michelle, Lynn, and I, as well as the counselors, were in shock as the buses left and our 97 first campers left us. We simply weren't prepared for the impact that their absence caused. We were also dealing with the collective experience of all our children leaving home, a death in the family, and the shock of considering what would come next.

The counselors instinctively formed a circle, with their arms over each other's shoulders. We then had a giant crying jag, punctuated by comments of how amazing this experience had been, and how the stronger the impact, the greater the emotional toll when it ends.

Since then, we have had 70 camp sessions for 7,700 campers. On the other hand, you can only have a first-time experience once. The stories that make up each camp can build, but there is nothing that ever again rivals the first time.

The camp director of Camp Sizanani is my friend, Kabelo Malefane (KB for short). I asked him to share his following experience:

KB's Story

Good day!

You know, at times, you hear of people saying they are not doing a JOB but are doing a calling. I think that I am one of the few who have been placed in this world for a very special purpose, which is to serve.

Do I ever regret leaving my nine-to-five job? Absolutely not, because when I finally said yes to my calling, I ended doing much more than what my nine-to-five could do.

We conduct life skills camps in South Africa. I remember one time that a camper came to me at the end of camp and said to me, "I would like to thank you Vochelli Kaybee for being the father that I have never had. During my stay at this camp, I have found in you everything that a father should be. Furthermore, I hope that you don't grow weary or tired along the way, because you have really changed my life by just spending a week at camp with you."

At first, I did not understand the message that this young man was conveying. Eventually, however, the thought of being acknowledged in such a way was humbling, as well as bigger than any paycheck I could have received. After this camp, it was very easy to resign from a nine-to-five routine and choose camps instead. Who can forget the friendships that come with every camp session?

Camp Vochellis serve so that others can live, which is why I love my calling. Having the opportunity to impact someone's life in this manner means a lot to me. The following is an article written by one of the young campers I came across as a camp counselor at Camp Echo in New York.

My name is Jon Rosenblum. I am honored to read my camper reflection out loud to the entire Echo family! Although I am sad to see the summer end, I am excited for my future at Echo. The transition from being a camper to becoming a counselor will be difficult, but I'm up for the challenge.

After my ninth summer at Echo, my final night as a camper is slowly coming to an end. Camp is a very special place for most people. As such, it is a privilege for both campers and counselors to spend their summers at Camp Echo. Campers and counselors create memories and bonds throughout their summers at this camp that will last forever. To this day, I hold a very special bond with past counselors and former bunkmates of mine.

For some campers and counselors, camp is a very hard place which to adjust. For me, it was a roller coaster. My first summer, my three sisters and my brother were with me in camp. They looked after me and made sure that I was able to have the best summer any young camper could imagine. As the summers went on, however, my siblings decided that their time had come, and that they would stop attending Camp Echo—their summer home. Having to adjust from having my siblings at camp, to becoming the only one in my family at camp was very difficult for me. My counselors and bunkmates, however, helped me get through this situation.

Growing up, I took everything for granted. Going into my 6th-grade summer, I had a counselor at Camp Echo, who was nicknamed KayBee. KayBee, who was born in Africa, had the privilege to come to America and share his stories. Despite our vastly different upbringings and the fact that we lived in two very different worlds, KayBee and I had a strong connection.

KayBee was someone to whom I would tell all my problems. He was always willing to listen and give advice. There was one night that had a lasting impression on me and changed my perspectives about a lot of things. My bunkmates and I were sitting around, when KayBee decided to tell us about his life and his hardships back in Africa. The stories were so moving that not only was I crying, but as I looked around the cabin, everyone was crying. It was then that I began to appreciate all that I have, as well as all that camp offers. We all have the opportunity to create lasting memories and bonds with our bunkmates and counselors from all around the world.

Being away from home is a very big step toward becoming independent and having courage. Camp teaches us life lessons and brings out qualities that some of us do not know that we have. For example, many of you don't know, but I have an adopted brother named Alex.

Losing both parents by the age of 16 is very difficult for anyone. My brother is probably one of the strongest people I have ever met. He has been through so much and no one in their life should ever have to experience what he experienced. For Alex, Camp Echo was a place where he found support and friendship in difficult times. I know that during the hardest part of his life, Camp Echo was his escape and the place where he felt safest.

Being a CIT this year has really helped me understand what camp is really about. The first four weeks of camp this summer, I had the best time of my life. Being able to wake up every day and put a smile on a young camper's face, while doing something I love, is definitely something that I will hold with me forever. It is my intention to return to Camp Echo for my 10th summer next year.

Standing here tonight and looking back on my past summers, it makes me think about my life, if I didn't come to camp. Would I be the person I am today? Would I be able to do the little things in life? Would I be friends with the people with whom I am friends? The answer to all these questions is most likely "no." There isn't enough gratitude in one lifetime to thank everyone who is a part of Camp Echo for everything they have done for me.

I'm reading this camper reflection to help make you realize that camp is just as important as anything else in life. In school, you learn science, English, math, social studies, and all the important, but often boring, things you need in life. In camp, you learn patience, compassion, reliability, self-improvement, courage, commitment, and reason, as well as every quality in between.

It is the aforementioned qualities that made me a better person, and it is these qualities that will make you a better person. Thank you Camp Echo for giving me a memorable nine summers as a camper. I hope that I am able to add a lot more summers to my life in this special setting. There is no other place that I would want to spend my summers and there are no other people with whom I would want to spend them.

About the Author

Michael Jacobus is a nationally-recognized camp professional and frequent presenter at camp conferences and retreats. He has an extensive background in youth development, staff training, operations and outdoor education. Michael has worked with private, public and non-profit groups including; the American Camp Association (ACA), Disney, the Boy Scouts of America (BSA), National Geographic, the Red Cross, Global Camps Africa, the Muscular Dystrophy Association, Nature Partners, Green Camps Initiative and the National Science Teachers Association.

He has been honored with the national award for Excellence in Sustainability Education from the BSA and has been recognized for Program Excellence and Excellence in Standards by the ACA.

Michael is an Eagle Scout who has drawn from a diverse background of experiences to become a dynamic industry leader. He has spent time as a ship captain on Lake Tahoe, a radio personality, pastor, magazine publisher, food broker & chemist. He's owned a screen-print & embroidery shop, designed two frisbee golf courses and taught drama, improv theatre and stagecraft at the elementary and university level. When he finds the time, he occasionally performs as an opera singer, (Tenor / Baritone), most recently singing at Christmastime as a member of the Disneyland Candlelight Choir.